Questions God Asks Us

Questions God Asks Us

Trevor Hudson

QUESTIONS GOD ASKS US

Upper Room Books® website: upperroombooks.com

Originally published in 2008 by Struik Christian Media (Pty) Ltd. under the title *Questions God Asks Us*. Published by permission of Three Streams Publishers © Struik Christian Media and Trevor Hudson.

Cover and interior design: Left Coast Design, Portland, Oregon / www.lcoast.com
Cover photo: Kamil Vojner, Photonica

LIBRARY OF CONGRESS CATALOGING-IN-PUBLICATION DATA

Hudson, Trevor, 1951–
Questions God asks us / by Trevor Hudson.
p. cm.
Includes bibliographical references
ISBN 978-0-8358-9990-1
1. Spiritual life—Christianity. I. Title.
BV4501.3.H82185 2009
248.4—DC22 2008042919

DEDICATION

To Debbie, Joni, and Mark
—for your deep love,
loyalty, and laughter

and

to Johann and Gail
—for your faithful friendship
over many years

#ACKNOWLEDGMENTS

As always, I am deeply in debt to a faithful circle of companions and colleagues. Without the gifts of their expertise and encouragement there would be no book at all. My heartfelt gratitude and appreciation goes to:

- Robin Pippin, Rita Collett, and the rest of the publishing team at Upper Room Books for all their efforts in making this book available;
- Lyn Meyer for placing her computer skills so generously at the service of this writing project;
- Bill Meaker who continues to mentor me in the ministry of writing for ordinary men and women;
- the members and staff of the Northfield Methodist Church with whom I have lived and explored these questions over the years;
- and finally, to Debbie Hudson whose everyday life with God embodies a rare faithfulness and integrity and realness.

CONTENTS

PREFACE

Have you ever stopped to think about the questions that God asks in the Bible? For many years I missed focusing on them. Perhaps it was because, like many others do, I thought that the Bible was just a book of answers. It existed to give me solutions to my everyday concerns and dilemmas. Then one day, several years ago, I realized that I might be approaching God and the Bible from the wrong direction. It was as if God said to me, "Trevor, rather than you always asking questions of me, start listening to the questions I have for you."

This realization was a critical turning point in my journey with God. Rather than always looking for answers in the Bible, I began to think more carefully about the questions that God asks. First, I did this in my own life of prayer and meditation.

Then I started to share the questions with others in small groups, on retreats, and in sermons. One day I decided to go further and write about them. You have in your hands the product of that decision taken several years ago.

I have often wondered why God would want to ask us questions. There could be several reasons. To begin with, God wants to enter into a conversational relationship with each of us. One way in which God shows this deep desire is by asking questions. They are the same questions that God asked the people of God throughout the Bible. When we start hearing them as addressed to us, we receive a glimpse into those things that God wants to talk about with us. Our answers draw us into a relationship of deeper sharing and intimacy with God.

Second, God gives greater dignity to us by allowing us to wrestle with the questions rather than simply giving us the answers. Recently I read that of the 183 questions that Jesus was asked in the four Gospels, he directly answered only three![1] (I will leave you to find out which three these are!) This little-known fact often surprises people who believe that Christianity always provides us with clear answers. Apparently, Jesus saw things quite differently. By asking us questions he wanted us to know that God really values what we think and feel.

Third, a question has greater power to transform us than a straightforward answer, especially when it comes from God who knows exactly what questions to ask. Certainly this has been my experience as I have lived with the ten questions in this book. They have invited me to look deeply and honestly into my heart. They have challenged me in my relationships. They have engaged me more realistically with the pain and suffering of our society. Somehow they have a way of getting inside of my life with a power to change me from the inside out.

As you set out on the journey of reading this book, let me offer some thoughts to guide you. You will notice that there are five questions from the First Testament and five from the Second Testament. I believe all these questions are asked by God, even those in the Second Testament. The basis of my conviction is that Jesus of Nazareth revealed God to us in the flesh. Remember his words: "Whoever has seen me has seen the Father" (NRSV). It follows that the questions Jesus asked people in the Gospels are the same questions that God addresses to each one of us.

You will also notice that each chapter ends with a section titled: "Answering God's Question." Here you will find suggestions about how you can personally explore God's question in the context of your own life. Do not forget that God wants a two-way relationship with you. You cannot have that kind of relationship without listening and speaking—or in other words, without dialogue. I hope that these ten questions will provide a starting point for a deep dialogue between God and yourself.

Finally, I hope that you might be able to explore these questions together with others. Something really good can happen in our lives when we share our personal experiences of engaging God's questions with other significant people in our lives. Some questions at the end of each chapter will help you use this book for group study. You may choose to use these in your personal reflection time and for group discussion.

As I wrestled with these questions in my own life, I found myself in a whole new world of conversational relationship and adventurous discipleship with God. I hope that this will also happen for you.

Chapter 1

Where Are You?

It is the first childhood game I remember playing. When I was small, our family lived in a tiny apartment. While my parents were busy, I would find a place to hide. There were not too many options. Sometimes I hid under a bed or behind the couch or in the clothes closet. Wherever it was, I would wait there, hoping to be missed. It was always a special moment when I heard Mom or Dad coming closer, calling out, "Where are you?"

This question seemed to touch me deeply. I can only try to guess why. Perhaps it assured me that my parents really loved me. Or it could be that it gave me a feeling of real belonging.

Maybe it just felt good to know that my absence had been noticed. I don't know for sure what the reason was. What I do know is that when my parents came looking for me, asking where I was, my heart was filled with a joyful delight. Little wonder I enjoyed playing the game so much.

The first question that God asked in the Bible was the same one my parents asked. It comes from the Creation story in the book of Genesis. You may remember the garden setting. Soon after our first ancestors had been created, they broke the one and only rule they had been given. The consequences, of course, were tragic—closeness with God and with each other was instantly destroyed by separation. Adam and Eve sewed fig leaves together to hide from each other, and they hid from God behind some bushes in the garden. Then we read these beautifully haunting words: "But the LORD God called to [them], 'Where are you?'"

I wonder how Adam and Eve felt when they heard God calling them. Were they afraid, wondering if God was going to pounce on them and punish them? After all, they must have known they had broken God's heart. Or did they feel something like I did when my parents came looking for me? Did God's question cause them to realize how much God longed for their company? I have often thought about these matters. My wonderings have shaped significantly the way I relate to God and live out my faith. Let me share with you what I mean by this.

God's Searching Heart

The other day I listened to someone tell the story of his spiritual journey. He described how, after years of searching, he had eventually found God. I had mixed feelings about his use of the phrase "found God." On the one hand, it contains a certain truth. We do search for God. On the other hand, we also try to hide away. But God is always trying to find us. This is the good news of the Creation story. When we hide from God, God comes seeking, calling out to each one of us, "Where are you?"

This question leads us into the searching heart of God. It reminds us that God always pursues us in love. Nothing can ever extinguish the flame in God's heart that burns to be in personal relationship with us—even when we mess up and get terribly lost. When God asks us where we are, it is as if God is saying to you and me, "Where are you? I miss you. My heart aches for you. I want to reconnect intimately with you. I grieve over the distance between us. I long for your companionship, and I will search for you until I find you."

Has it ever struck you that this is the same message that Jesus shared about God in many places in the Gospels? One of my favorite stories is the one that he told about the woman who had ten coins and lost one. Remember what she did? She lit a lamp, fetched a broom, and began to sweep. Until when? Until it got dark? No. Until she got tired? No. Until the broom began to wear out? No. She swept and swept and swept until she found the lost coin. She swept for as long as was necessary. There are no limits on God's seeking love. None!

Nothing can ever extinguish the flame in God's heart that burns to be in personal relationship with us.

Jesus' parable wonderfully illustrates God's searching heart. God, says Jesus, is like this woman. God looks for each one of us until we are found. We are loved with an unlimited love, with an everlasting love, with a love that will never let us go. God passionately desires an intimate relationship with each one of us. Our hearts have been fashioned for this divine connection, and nothing but a close and personal relationship with God will ever satisfy our deepest longings.

Meditate on this question, "Where are you?" Allow it to lead you deeper into God's searching heart. Imagine God this very moment thinking of you with persistent longing. Bask in the sunshine of this blazing love; let its powerful rays warm your heart. If God's love does not seem real to you, ask God to give you this knowledge—in your heart not your head. Frederick Buechner puts it well: "If you have never known the power of God's love, then maybe it is because you have never asked to know it—I mean really asked, expecting an answer."[1]

Coming Out of Hiding

One day a man went to see a doctor because he was very depressed. The doctor examined him and found his physical condition to be in good shape. So he said to the man, "There is a circus in town with a marvelous clown by the name of Grimaldi. Everybody who goes to see him laughs. Why don't you do the same thing? He'll make you laugh and then you will feel much better."

The patient replied, "Doctor, that won't help. I am Grimaldi."[2]

A lot of us are like Grimaldi. We hide who we really are. We hide from those around us and from God. Sometimes we may even try to hide from ourselves as well. We hide because we believe that if we are ever known for who we really are, we will not be acceptable. So we go through much of our lives continually projecting images of who we are not. Behind these facades there exists the real person—the real me—but who sometimes is so well hidden that we may not even know our true thoughts or feelings.

We hide ourselves in different ways. We put on a smiling face when we are sad. We try to look confident when we are afraid. We act as if we have it all together when it's all falling apart. We go through the motions of believing when we doubt. We feign interest when we honestly don't care. In the words of the Adam and Eve story, we cover up our nakedness with the fig leaves of pretense. Not surprisingly, our relationships with God and other people are often characterized by a sad superficiality and lack of intimacy. Pretend people have pretend relationships.

God's question invites us to come out of hiding, to take off our fig leaves, and to become more real. Our relationships with God and others change for the better when we begin to do this. When we come before our Creator in simple honesty, there is a response on God's part that helps us to know that we are loved. God lets us know that we are accepted, just as we are. As a result, we don't need to pretend so much any more. We can come out from where we have been hiding and start to relate more openly and freely. It's quite liberating!

God's question invites us to come out of hiding, to take off our fig leaves, and to become more real.

My own journey has taught me this. I came out of hiding for the first time when I was a teenager. Walking down a dark street in Port Elizabeth one night, I shared with God what was going on in my life, good and bad. "God," I prayed, "I give my whole life to you." Since that evening I have needed to come out of hiding many more times. Each time it has seemed like opening up to God another hidden layer of my life. And every time I do this, I find myself experiencing God's love in a deeper way than before. May this be your experience as you respond to God's question, "Where are you?"

Making God's Love Real

This question also challenges us to make God's love real for others. We are surrounded by people who find it hard to believe that they matter to God. Often these men and women have suffered a great deal. Their lives have been scarred by oppression or tragedy or rejection or abuse or some other form of deep hurt. They feel that God does not care. These are people for whom God's searching heart aches. But they need someone to put flesh and blood on the divine compassion before they can experience God's loving question, "Where are you?"

The following story by Renée Altson has guided my efforts in learning how to love those who are hurting deeply. This testimony comes from her book *Stumbling toward Faith.* As a child Renée was raped repeatedly by her father while he sang Christian choruses and recited the Lord's Prayer. Later, her addicted and homeless mother abandoned her. Superficial responses by Christians to the pain she was experiencing only deepened her sense of alienation. When she had almost given up on Christianity, someone entered her life who made God's love real. She describes the experience like this:

> He lived God's love into me through his life, through his love. He cared about me, was willing to spend time with me, and embraced me in all of my fractured disbelief and doubt. He didn't give me pat answers. In fact, many times he didn't give me any answers. Rather he gave me permission to be without them—an indescribable gift. He gave me the space to ask questions, to be honest, to struggle, to grieve.
>
> I felt the freedom to be half-finished. I felt the freedom to cry, to mourn for all I had lost. I felt that God loved me in the midst of my half-finished mourning, that He heard me when I cried. I felt that love through my friend, a love that was gentle and patient and playful.

> He helped bring life and hope to me. He saw my deadness and my brokenness and entered into it instead of trying to talk me out of it. He acknowledged my despair and then quietly, without words, pointed the way to something bigger than him. He pointed me to springtime and light and life, all the while acknowledging the winter, the darkness, the pain.[3]

Can you glimpse how we can make God's love real? When we can be there with those who suffer, we bring God's love to them. We also experience God's love more deeply. If, however, we are unable to show love and acceptance like this, perhaps we still need to know God's love more deeply ourselves. When we are found by God, divine love flows naturally into the way we relate to others.

Answering God's Question

Where are you? God longs to be in one-on-one conversation with us. And so God takes the initiative in coming toward us and asking this question. Think about this for a moment. We are not starting the conversation with God from scratch. God has already begun it. We just need to plug into the conversation that is already going on. One way for us to do this is to respond to this question. Here are some suggestions.

Begin by telling God what is going on in your life at the moment. Share with God your deepest longings, your joys, your sorrow, your shame, your fears. You may argue that it is a waste of time to tell God these things. After all, surely God knows everything already. However, it's not a question of giving new information to God but a matter of coming out of hiding and learning to speak openly with God about everything in your life and then experiencing the closeness that this kind of transparency brings to your relationship with God.

You may also want to respond to the challenge of this question: to make God's love real. The God we meet in the Bible looks for every human being, no matter who he or she is or what he or she has done. Each person has a special place in God's searching heart. God's dream for our world is that every human being will come to know that place—especially those who suffer and are in deep pain. You have a role to play in making God's dream come true. Obviously, you cannot reach out to everyone who is suffering. But in your conversation with God, you can ask, "Lord, who falls within my care? To whom can I bring your love?"

Once more I remind you that God desires an intimate relationship with you. May your willingness to be in conversation with God by answering this question open the door to an intimacy that goes beyond your wildest imaginings!

Questions for Small Groups

1. Where are you, at the moment, in your relationship journey with God?
2. How do you sometimes hide from God and from those around you?
3. When did you first become aware of God's personal love for you?
4. Who has made God's love real for you? How did he or she do this?

Chapter 2

Where Is Your Brother?

A few weeks ago I conducted the funeral of a young man in his twenties. He had gone to his company's office party. Being one of the youngest and newest employees, the man found his colleagues challenging him to down some mixed cocktails. When he climbed into his car to drive home, he was in no state to drive; but none of his colleagues felt it was his or her responsibility to restrain or stop him. On the way home, on an open stretch of road, he fell asleep at the wheel. The car overturned, killing him instantly. His family was devastated by this senseless death.

I have thought a lot about this tragedy. It raises many questions. Were the young man's colleagues to blame in any way for his death? Should they have prevented him from getting into the car? Do they have blood on their hands? Are they blameless for what happened? Questions like these introduce a difficult, complex, and challenging issue: What is our responsibility toward each other? Should we mind our own business, not care about what takes place around us, and let everyone be accountable for his or her own life? Or do we have a God-given responsibility to ensure the well-being of our loved ones and friends, our neighbors and our enemies, and even our world?

Our second question addresses this issue. It comes from the familiar story of Cain and Abel, the first children of Adam and Eve. You can read about it in the fourth chapter of Genesis. Both of them worshiped God. Cain offered on the altar the fruits of the field, while Abel offered a lamb from his flock. For reasons that we can only wonder about, God accepted Abel's sacrifice and rejected Cain's. Soon afterward, in a fit of jealous rage Cain killed his brother. Immediately God appeared on the scene to ask Cain the question, "Where is your brother?" (v. 9).

This question invites us to consider our responsibility toward one another from at least three different angles. None of these invitations is easy. We tend to shy away from their uncomfortable challenges. Nonetheless, I do hope that you will consider each one of them seriously. Those who have responded positively to these invitations have found themselves transformed, and their lives and faith have become far more meaningful. Perhaps this will also happen for you and me as we look closer and respond to the challenges the invitations bring to our lives.

Our Responsibility toward Our Neighbors

First of all, this question invites us to recognize our responsibility toward our neighbors. These neighbors include our families, our friends and colleagues, the people who live next door, and those we meet as we go about our daily lives. They are all part of the human family to which you and I belong; we are all connected. When God asks us, "Where is your brother?" these people should immediately come to mind. In effect, God is asking, "Are you willing to take some responsibility for the well-being of these men and women with whom you spend time on a regular basis?"

Cain, you may remember, sidestepped this invitation. When God asked about his brother's whereabouts, he had a wonderful opportunity to model what it meant to be a responsible member of God's human family. He could have said to God, "Lord, I killed my brother. I have done a terrible thing. I have sinned against you and your family. Please forgive me. I will try to make amends in whatever way I can." Imagine, if you can, the creative and life-giving consequences that would have flowed throughout the world from this kind of response.

However, Cain's answer displayed a flat refusal to take any responsibility toward his brother. "I don't know. Am I my brother's keeper?" Bible scholars point out that the Hebrew word that Cain used for "keeper" was also used in relation to animals. Shepherds were called "keepers" of goats and sheep and other kinds of livestock. In other words, Cain's callous response to God's question could be roughly translated into something like: "How should I know where my brother is? After all, he really was a bit of an animal. Am I supposed to take care of animals?" He stubbornly refused to be accountable in any way for the well-being of his brother as a fellow human being.

But, you may be thinking, *surely my neighbors need to take responsibility for their own lives.* Certainly they must. We all need to take responsibility for our own lives. Indeed, for some matters, we and we alone are responsible. Think, for example, of the choices and decisions that we make every day. No one else can be held accountable for them, except us. Nevertheless, God's question seems to imply that in certain respects we are accountable for what happens to those around us. Our job is to try to work out what our responsibility involves.

Our lives are deeply bound up with each other's. Whether we acknowledge it or not, our actions do affect those around about us.

Let us go back to the story of the young man who was killed in the car accident. He made certain choices for which he alone was responsible. He chose to go to the office party. He chose to accept the challenge to drink the mixed cocktails. No one else can be blamed for these decisions. But his senior colleagues were not blameless. They abused their influence in getting him to drink. They could have restrained him from driving home in his drunken condition. The fact is that our lives are bound up with each other's. Whether we acknowledge it or not, our actions do affect those around about us. God's question to each one of us—"Where is your brother?" or "Where is your sister?"—challenges us to recognize this fact.

Our Responsibility toward Our Enemies

Second, this question invites us to recognize our responsibility toward our enemies. But this recognition will take place only if we are also willing to see our enemies as our brothers and sisters. Our usual tendency is just the opposite. We tend to demonize them. They are different to us. They are bad, and we are good. They are not worth bothering with. Sometimes we may even wish that they were dead. The Bible, however, is clear about one thing. God does care about them and desires our acknowledgment that we and they belong to the same human family. We find this very hard to do, especially if we have been deeply hurt by someone.

This is precisely the journey that God wanted Cain to go on. Cain obviously saw Abel as a threat. Why else would he have murdered him? He must have had a deep resentment in his heart toward Abel. Perhaps Cain felt that his parents loved Abel more than they loved him. Perhaps he was jealous about Abel being more gifted and successful. Perhaps he had been badly hurt by Abel in some way when they were growing up together. Whatever the reason for the enmity between them, Abel had become Cain's enemy. God's question challenged Cain to see Abel as his brother.

A chilling legend[1] makes a similar point. One night during the Middle Ages, two warriors in full armor were riding along separate paths, each thinking there was no one else around for miles. Their paths crossed, and the warriors came upon each other in the darkness of a heavily wooded forest. Both were startled, and each misinterpreted the movements of the other as gestures of hostility. So they began to fight, each believing he was under attack and must defend himself. The conflict grew more intense until one knight succeeded in knocking the other off his horse. With one mighty effort, he drove his lance through the fallen man's heart. He then dismounted and limped over to the adversary he had just killed. He pulled back the face mask and there, to his horror, in the pale moonlight he recognized his brother. He had mistaken a family member for an enemy and had destroyed him.

The way we choose to see others makes a huge difference in the way we behave toward them, especially if they are our enemies.

Can we learn to see our enemy as a brother or sister? The story of Cain and Abel reminds us that when we have a mindset that sees each other as the enemy, destruction follows. But when we choose to see our enemies as fellow human beings, the opposite can take place. The way we choose to see others makes a huge difference in the way we behave toward them, especially if they are our enemies. We do not usually feel much responsibility toward those whom we dislike or hate. However, if we make a deliberate choice to see someone as belonging to the same human family as we do, we are more likely to treat them in a humane and respectful way.

Would you agree that we all have enemies? Sometimes we struggle to admit this. We want to think that we really love everyone and that everyone loves us. This is highly unlikely. Most of us have people in our lives whom we do not like or who do not like us. Enemies are those toward whom we feel hostile and who sometimes feel hostile toward us. Often our enemy can be within our own family, just like it was for Cain. Through the question "Where is your brother?" God invites us to recognize that we have a responsibility toward that person. We take our first step in choosing to acknowledge this when we begin to see our enemy as our brother or sister.

Our Responsibility toward the Wider World

Third, the question invites us to recognize our responsibility toward the wider world. You may feel totally overwhelmed by this challenge. Do we not often think or say something like: "I am just an ordinary person. There is nothing that I can do about the big issues of corruption and crime and unemployment and poverty and violence and AIDS that threaten to destroy the fabric of our life together. I didn't cause them, and therefore I don't need to do anything about them. It's up to those in authority to sort out the situation." Ring a bell?

Let me share a story that challenges us to think a little differently. On September 18, 2002, a six-year-old girl was raped in Alexandra township in Johannesburg. She was left for dead. Mercifully she was found and taken to a nearby hospital. The nurses named her Lerato (which means "love" in Sesotho). Lerato has survived, but no human being will ever know the inner trauma and anguish that she has experienced.

Lerato's story deeply touched a good friend of mine. Together with a group of men he organized a Men's Repentance March. This was a public march before God and the community of Alexandra, confessing what men have done to women and children in South Africa. Almost 350 men put on sackcloth, covered themselves with ashes, wrote the sins of men on cardboard nailed to wooden crosses, which they then carried in silence through the streets of Alexandra. When they came to the place where Lerato had been raped, they knelt in the dust and repented publicly before God and the community. They prayed for God to deliver men from their sinfulness, to heal them in their brokenness, and to transform the nation.[2]

I was deeply moved by the action of my friend. Like many other men, I had read the story about Lerato. I had also been horrified by what had happened to her. However, that was where my response stopped. My friend went a few steps further. He knew that such evil could not go unchallenged. Something had to be done to highlight the depravity that threatens to destroy our nation. Even though he had not personally committed the sin against Lerato, he was willing to take responsibility in some way for the manner in which men often treat women and children in this country. He had engaged God's question "Where is your brother?" with his actions of identification and protest.

God continues to ask us this same question. Few questions are more relevant against the background of our traumatized society.

God continues to ask us this same question. Few questions are more relevant against the background of our traumatized society. I believe that of all the horrible sins that plague our life together, the most deadly is indifference. We do not want to get involved in the suffering that happens around us. We refuse to take responsibility in any way for the evil that takes place in our midst. We may be moved by the pain of people, like I was when I read the story of Lerato, but we avoid taking any action that will engage us directly with the sources of evil. However, this could change if we are willing to engage God's question.

Answering God's Question

"Where is your brother?" "Where is your sister?" Will you hear God's question as a call to give thought to your responsibility toward others?

Begin with the circle of your family, friends, and colleagues. While they are responsible for their own choices, reflect on how you can contribute to their well-being. Be careful that your caring does not encourage destructive behavior. Sometimes this can happen when a child or a parent struggles with some form of addiction. Think carefully about how you try to help them. It may be important to let them experience certain painful consequences of their actions in order to come to the point of realizing that they really have a problem. Talk to God about these things, and discuss them with others whom you can trust, if you need to.

Now think of someone you consider to be an enemy. It may be someone in your own family, a neighbor across the street, a colleague in the workplace, or someone you view as an oppressor or exploiter. Own your feelings toward this person and offer him or her honestly to God. Ask God to help you begin choosing to see this person in a new way. He or she is not all bad, and you are not all good. Pray that you may accept him or her as your brother or sister in the human family. Look with the eyes of your heart at this person as someone who has also been given breath by the same Creator who gave you breath. Let your behavior toward this person be influenced by the new way you see him or her.

Lastly, you may want to reflect on your wider responsibility toward the world. Clearly you cannot take responsibility for all the pain and misery and suffering that permeates society today. But you can ask God, "Lord, who is the suffering brother or sister that I need to recognize? To what human cry in my broader community must I listen? Where are you calling me to respond to the human need around me? Where can I contribute to the common good through prayer, protest, and practical action?" As people and places come to your mind, speak to God about them.

God has one human family to which we all belong. Few questions help us reflect on this truth more than the question that God asked Cain. In fact, I believe that our future depends on whether we engage it or not.

Questions for Small Groups

1. What were your thoughts and feelings when you read the incident about the young man who got drunk at the party and was later killed in the car accident?
2. How do you work out the extent and limits of your responsibility toward others?
3. How do you respond to the gospel challenge of acknowledging enemies as brothers or sisters in the human family?
4. In what ways is God calling you to exercise responsibility toward others at the moment?

Chapter 3

What Is That in Your Hand?

A Christian legend relates the thought that God sends each person into the world with a special message to deliver, with a special song to sing for others, with a special act of love to bestow. No one else can bring our message, sing our song, or offer our love. Only we can. This legend reminds us that each of us has something of value to offer to the life of our world—something that can make this world a much better place.[1]

However, you may struggle with this idea, especially when it comes to the challenge of tackling some of the problem areas in our society. When we look at the conditions that cause so much human suffering today—poverty, AIDS, addiction, crime, joblessness, sickness, loneliness—and when challenged to make a creative difference, we often put forward excuses why we cannot.

Our excuses vary and usually revolve around the lack of suitable abilities or resources. We don't have the necessary qualifications. We don't have enough money. We don't have the available time. We don't have the needed skills. We don't have significant influence. We don't have adequate knowledge. We don't have the required energy. And so, armed with one or another of these reasons, we justify our lack of action and try to escape our personal responsibility in building a better world.

In many respects we are like Moses. You may remember the story of the burning bush when God called him to free the Hebrews from their oppression. Before Moses said yes, he tried to sidestep his calling with a whole list of excuses. They sound a lot like those we sometimes make when God calls us. Here is my loosely paraphrased version of his five excuses. Can you recognize any from your own experience?

- I'm nobody.
- I don't know enough about God.
- What happens if I fail?
- I don't have what it takes.
- Someone else could do it better.

In the midst of all these excuses, God asked Moses, "What is that in your hand?"(Exod. 4:2). It was a question aimed at helping Moses recognize that he already had all the resources he needed to fulfill God's calling. At that moment Moses was holding a staff. God wanted to use this simple stick to liberate a nation. When we make available to God whatever we are holding in our hands, we will always be astounded by what God can do with it.

What is that in your hand right at this moment? God wants to use you and what's in your hand to change this world for the better. You may be unsure of your answer, but I suggest that every one of us has three things in our hands right now.

Our Abilities

All of us have certain abilities in our hands—whatever they happen to be: running a business, using the computer, managing projects, resolving conflict, working with figures, managing money, coaching sports, offering hospitality, and so on. God is able to use them for the sake of the common good. We need to acknowledge what we do well and invest whatever it is in God's work of mending our broken world, even when we believe our talents are rather insignificant.

I have had to learn in my own life that nothing is too small for God to use. Ever since I first gave my life to God, I have wanted to be a channel of God's healing love. However, I was unsure how this could happen. Then, in my early twenties, I took part in a three-month leadership training program. One day the participants were asked, in small groups, to think about each other's lives and to say what we valued about them. The exercise started well. Each person took a turn to listen while the rest of us affirmed what he could do well. I was the last. The group was quiet for some time. Finally, someone broke the silence and said, "Trevor, I think you are a good listener."

To be honest, I was a little disappointed. My colleagues had been affirmed for seemingly stronger talents: "excellent people skills," "able to delegate well," "capacity for visionary leadership," "excellent managerial ability," and the like. In comparison, just being able to listen sounded quite tame. Nonetheless, two members of the group still had to give their impressions of me. Perhaps they would notice something more exciting. The next one said, "I agree. I think you can listen quite well."

Far from feeling affirmed, I now felt a bit deflated. When the last person said the same thing, I wanted to curl up in a corner and die. Listening didn't sound like that great a gift. However, to this day, I can still remember that night, kneeling at the side of my bed and offering to God what was in my hand. "Dear God, thank you for this listening ability. I give it to you. I commit myself to develop it as much as I can. Will you please use it to make a difference in the lives of others." Looking back now, I am deeply moved by the opportunities that God has given me to use the ability to listen. It has given my life tremendous meaning and value.

What ability do you hold in your hand? Please don't compare it with what others have. It may be big or small, but God has uniquely gifted you for a specific purpose. You already possess what God wants to use to bless others. Thank God for your ability; commit yourself to develop it further and to employ it in the service of others. When we use whatever is in our hand with courage and compassion, we begin to contribute toward the building of a better world for all, even if the only thing we can do well is listen!

God has uniquely gifted you for a specific purpose. You already possess what God wants to use to bless others.

Our Life Experience

All of us have life experience in our hands. Of course, this life experience differs vastly from one person to another. It usually includes lessons we have learned while growing up, the work we have done, the mistakes we have made, the successes we have achieved, and, perhaps most importantly from God's perspective, the painful things we have suffered. Our life experience represents a huge resource for God's use in healing a hurting world. As we learn from many Bible stories, the way God uses us is often related to the ups and downs we have gone through.

Moses' life again vividly illustrates this truth. Don't you sometimes wonder why God chose him? After all, he seemed an unlikely candidate for the job God wanted done. Ever since Moses had killed an Egyptian, he had been on the run. For forty years he had hidden in the desert, looking after sheep. You don't develop much of a resume doing that. Surely someone else was better qualified. However, when we dig a little deeper into Moses' life experience, we begin to see why God called him.

First of all, there was Moses' childhood experience. When Pharaoh ordered the Hebrew midwives to kill all the Jewish male babies, Moses' mother hid him where Pharaoh's daughter bathed. The princess found him, and he grew up in Pharaoh's household with all the privileges that brought. No doubt he received an excellent education, together with an insider's understanding of the workings of power in Pharaoh's court. Think about how this knowledge would later be put to good use when he went to Pharaoh and confronted him with God's demands.

Then, there was Moses' experience of working for forty years as a shepherd in the desert. Consider the many survival skills he must have acquired, skills that would one day prove invaluable when leading a sometimes stubborn and resistant people through the same difficult terrain, skills that he could have learned nowhere except through personal experience. As Bruce Larson points out, Moses' time of living among the Bedouins uniquely trained him to lead the Israelites through a murderous, punishing desert that showed no mercy toward human beings or animals.[2]

Third, Moses had the benefit of the spiritual preparation that took place during these long, lonely years. Shepherding has always been a lonely occupation. Solitude and silence, we know, has the power to transform us. It provides space for personal reflection, self-examination, and encounter with God. Judging by Moses' response to the burning bush, his life experience was no exception in this regard. During his time alone in the desert he seems clearly to have developed a keen spiritual sensitivity that would strengthen him in the difficult years ahead.

From the moment we were born . . . God has been forming us to be a difference-making member of the human family.

Can you see how, from childhood through to adulthood, Moses' life experience prepared him for God's use in an amazing way? It is the same for you and me. From the moment we were born, through all the troubles and tensions of growing up, the adventures of young adulthood, through all our different jobs, all the joys and sorrows we have known, God has been forming us to be a difference-making member of the human family. What we have to do, however, is to offer God the life experience we bring in our hands.

Our Inadequacy

All of us have in our hands our own inadequacy, which should not make us feel bad. The tasks to which God may call us often seem impossible. Certainly this was true for Moses. Imagine how he felt when God called him to demand the release of the Israelite slaves from one of the great powers of the ancient world. Totally inadequate! No wonder he made excuses. Indeed, Moses' story reminds us that one of the clearest marks of God's call is that it leaves us feeling totally inadequate.

What matters, however, is how we choose to deal with our inadequacy. Several options face us. We can allow it to paralyze us. Our excuses then end up having the last word. Or we can let our inadequacy lead us into a greater dependence on God. This is what Moses chose to do. He took seriously God's promise to be with him and began to follow God's call, one step at a time. Let us resolve to do the same.

Recently I led a retreat around the call of Moses. While preparing for the final session I wrote this poem. It's based on one that I read many years ago, but I cannot trace it. Perhaps you can identify with it.

The Lord said to me—Go
And I said—Who, me?
And God said—Yes, you!
But I answered:
  I feel really inadequate
  I don't have the gifts
  I don't know enough
And the Lord said—You're stalling!

The Lord said—Go

And I answered:
But what happens if I fail?
I don't have what it takes.
What will others say?
Send someone else!
And the Lord said—Stop wriggling!

The Lord said—Go
And I said:
But I am on my own
Who will help me?
It's too scary
And the Lord said—Do you think I'll be far away?

And the Lord said—Go
And I shrugged and said:
Okay, Lord, have it your way
Here I am
Send me.

Answering God's Question

So what's that in your hand? Answering God's question could open up an exciting journey for you. Think about it for a moment. God wants to use whatever resources are already in your hand to bring hope and healing to a hurting world—just as God used Moses' resources 3,200 years ago. But first you need a willingness to converse with God around this question. Are you ready?

Begin by being honest with God about some of the excuses you make when you sense God is calling you to make the world a better place. Getting real about your resistances often clears the way for a deeper engagement with God. Once you have done this, imagine God whispering to you, "As I promised to be with Moses, so I promise to be with you. My presence and power will always be available to you. No difficult experience can separate you from me. And whatever you bring in your hands, I will use."

With this assurance of God's promise echoing in your heart and mind, speak with God about what you bring in your hands. Name your abilities; give thanks for them; offer them to God. Reflect on the richness of your life experience. Tell God about the pain you have gone through. You could find hidden there the seeds of the important things that God has for you to do. Above all, share with God your feelings of inadequacy, because this will be the area where you most experience God's power as you step out to follow God's calling.

Let me remind you one last time that God has something beautiful for you to do in this world, just like the legend suggested.

Sharing that message, singing that song, and offering that act of love will bring tremendous fulfillment. It will also enrich the lives of others. May answering God's question help you know that you already possess whatever you need to make this legend come true.

Questions for Small Groups

1. What is your favorite excuse to avoid the challenges of trying to make the world a better place?
2. Name one ability that others value and appreciate in your life.
3. Describe one resource that you bring to others because of your unique life experience.
4. How would you like to have God use you to make a creative difference in our world?

Chapter 4

What Is Your Name?

One teacher from my school years stands out in my memory with much affection. His name was Mr. Vosloo. He was my fifth-grade classroom teacher and also my rugby coach. I liked him because he did something that no other teacher had done until then, something very simple. In a school where we were addressed only by our surnames, he was the first teacher ever to call me by my first name. One day, when he was coaching us on the rugby field, he called out to me, "Trevor." Names are important. Think about it for a moment. We come into this world without them. They are the first gifts we receive from our parents. More often than not they are chosen with great thought and care. We have them until we die. They are the way in which we are recognized, loved, and remembered. Perhaps this is why we like to be greeted by name. Certainly it was the reason why such joy came over my young heart on that rugby field over forty-five years ago.

Your name described who you were and what you were meant to become.

In the culture of biblical times, names carried a much greater importance. They were not just ways in which people were called, which is the general purpose they serve today. Names were given to describe the essence of a person's character. They also symbolized the hopes, expectations, and dreams that the parents had for their children. Your name described who you were and what you were meant to become. In those ancient days one of the most important things a parent could do was to name his or her child.

Keep these thoughts about the importance of names in your mind as we explore God's next question. It comes from a well-known episode in the life of a famous Old Testament character by the name of Jacob. You can read the story in Genesis 32. Jacob was on his way home to meet his brother, Esau, from whom he had been alienated for twenty years. The last time he had seen Esau was when he had cheated him out of his blessing, and Esau had vowed to kill him. Esau's coming to meet him with four hundred armed men made him understandably anxious. Jacob sent his family ahead and went down to the river Jabbok on his own. There, we are told, he wrestled with God throughout the night. That is when God asked him, "What is your name?" (Gen. 32:27).

When Jacob answered this question, he experienced a miracle of inner change. One writer has called this riverbank moment Jacob's conversion experience.[1] It was the moment when he faced up honestly to who he was, experienced God's blessing, and in the process became more truly God's person. Since our faith journeys are made up of many conversion experiences, let us engage this question. It can help us become honest about who we are and receive the blessing that God wants to give. You and I can be sure that when this happens, it will help us become the person God wants us to be. We will even be given, just like Jacob, a new name that will indicate God's will and purpose for our lives.

Facing Up to Who We Are

The miracle of inner change requires that we face up honestly to ourselves. We see this clearly in Jacob's life. The Hebrew meaning of the name Jacob was "cheat" or "deceiver." Quite literally, his name meant "to grab someone's heel." Jacob certainly lived up to his name. He deceived his father, his brother, and his father-in-law. He lived his life by trickery and deceit. The turning point in his journey began to take place only when he faced up to God's question "What is your name?" and became honest about who he really was.

For over twenty years Jacob had deliberately avoided using his own name. You can see this in the details of his story in Genesis. Once, when he brought his father some roasted goat, he pretended to be his brother. He put on his brother's clothing, covered his arms and neck with goat hair, and said to his father who could not see, "I am Esau." Another time he met the woman of his dreams at the well and introduced himself as a relative of her father and a son of Rebecca. He obviously battled using his own name, which seems to describe in a symbolic way Jacob's deep struggle to accept himself, warts and all.

Can you see now how significant it was for Jacob to answer God's question? When he told God, "My name is Jacob," he was acknowledging who he was and what he had become. He was being honest with himself and with God for the first time. He was becoming real. No longer was he pretending to be Esau in disguise or merely his mother's son. Now he was acknowledging who he had been and what he had done. He was Jacob, who had cheated his brother, deceived his father, and tricked his father-in-law. It was a moment of radical self-honesty that opened up the way for God to give him a new name.

God cannot transform us if we do not willingly reveal all of ourselves.

Jacob reminds us that if we want to experience inner change, we must tell God who we truly are, willingly revealing all of ourselves. We need to acknowledge in God's presence those parts of our lives that need transformation—our anger and fears, our critical and gossipy sides, our prejudices, our dishonesty and deception, our lustful desires and addictions. God never gatecrashes our lives with the Spirit's transforming power. God confronts us with a question that challenges us to become totally honest and real. God asks us, "What is your name?"

Experiencing God's Blessing

When we face up to ourselves, we experience God's blessing. The God of the Bible loves to bless, and these blessings come in different and surprising ways. Often they are connected to what we need most. Sometimes God blesses us with the gift of forgiveness or with a deep affirmation of our worth or with a new infilling of divine power or with a renewed sense of belonging or with a fresh awareness of God's Spirit. All these blessings contribute to the miracle of inner change. However, before we can receive them, we need to share with God who we are and what we have done. We need to tell God our name.

We can see how this works in Jacob's relationship with God. Step back for a moment into his life story. When we meet him in Genesis 32, we are told that he was frightened and worried. His deceptive past had caught up with him. Alone for the first time in ages, he went down to the Jabbok River. There he wrestled with a mysterious stranger. In the midst of this wrestling match, an important exchange took place between him and God. First Jacob cried out, "I will not let you go unless you bless me." Immediately God responded, "What is your name?"

If we want God to bless us, we need to face up to ourselves honestly.

Do you see what was happening here? Jacob, in crisis, knew that it was God's nature to bless, and he needed that blessing. His cry requesting God's blessing was passionate, desperate, and demanding. However, God did not immediately bless him; God wanted to know his name. There needed to be an honest disclosure about who he was. For Jacob to receive the blessing that God wanted to give, he had to be willing to come clean.

There is a clear message here for those of us in crisis and in need of God's blessing. We must tell God our names and share with God who we really are and what we have done. Usually we want our relationship with God to work the other way around. Like Jacob, we want to know God's name. Often this indicates that we want a tame God whom we can manage for our ends. We do not want God to be too surprising or unpredictable or wild. Nor do we want to go into too many details about the mess in our lives. But that is not the way God works. If we want God to bless us, we need to face up to ourselves honestly.

This happened for a member of our congregation just a few weeks ago. He came to see me because, in his own words, his life was falling apart. He had been involved in a lifestyle of infidelity, prostitution, and drug-taking. Finally, things had caught up with him. He desperately wanted God's blessing. I asked him to go home and write out a personal inventory of all that he had done. When we got together again, I asked him to read this out in the presence of God. We spoke about how he could begin to make some amends for what he had done. Then I laid my hands on his head and prayed for God to bless him with the gifts of forgiveness and new beginnings. I have seen him a few times since this moment. While he is still dealing with the consequences of his actions, there is a wonderful newness about him. He has experienced God's blessing.

Receiving Our New Name

The miracle of inner change involves one more aspect, perhaps the most important, certainly the most wonderful: God gives you and me a new name. When we face up to ourselves before God, along with whatever other blessings we may receive we are always given a new identity. This new identity tells us that no matter who we are or what we have done, God has a new future for us. We are not defined forever by our past sins and failures. As someone once said to me, "Trevor, a new name can make you a new person."

No matter who we are, or what we have done, God has a new future for us.

We witness the power of a new name in the life of Jacob. Let us return to his story one last time. When Jacob acknowledged his own name before God, God said to him, "Your name will no longer be Jacob, but Israel." In those days the name "Israel" carried powerful meaning. In effect, by giving Jacob the name Israel, God was saying to him, "You are no longer Jacob the cheat, the deceiver, the one who always skirts the issue. From now on you are Israel, the one in whom God rules, the one whose life is now tied up with God's purposes, the one who is able to face hard things head-on."

Amazingly, Jacob immediately began to live up to his new name. In fact we do not see him tricking or deceiving again. There was a new humility in him. When he eventually faced his brother, he bowed before him seven times; and they were finally reconciled after all those years. There was also a new courage. He was now prepared to meet Esau himself, instead of sending others in his place. Jacob was no longer an escapist; he had changed from being someone who always tried to evade hard issues to being someone who was willing to face up to matters. His new name had empowered a new way of living.

But, you may want to ask, "How do I find out what my new name is?" Obviously we cannot physically imitate Jacob's experience alongside the Jabbok River. Nonetheless, God does have a new name for each one of us. This new name reminds us of who we really are, to whom we belong, and what our true calling is. It is tucked away in some words, written centuries after the life of Jacob, by someone who was very close to Jesus. Listen for it carefully. "How great is the love the Father has lavished on us, that we should be called children of God! And that is what we are" (1 John 3:1).

We are God's beloved! That is our true name, our deepest identity, our divine calling.

We are God's beloved! That is our true name, our deepest identity, our divine calling. Some reading these words may find this extremely hard to believe—for many reasons. We may find ourselves struggling with negative images about ourselves. Perhaps we struggle with a low sense of self-worth and poor self-esteem. Or we may feel that we have sinned too greatly to be worthy of God's love. Or perhaps in the light of some terrible and unfair tragedy, we believe God is against us. Yet the truth of the gospel is that each one of us is deeply loved, accepted, and forgiven by God in Jesus Christ. Indeed, we have been God's beloved from the beginning of time.

If you find it difficult to hear God naming you as beloved, I invite you to try this simple prayer exercise. It is one that has helped me in those dark moments when I have struggled to know myself as someone deeply loved by God. It goes like this: Take some time to be alone with God. Ask God's Spirit to be with you and to assure you of your new name, "God's beloved." Imagine yourself kneeling before the cross on which Jesus hung. As you look at him, he looks at you and whispers the words, "You are God's beloved. Look at my cross. See how much you are loved, accepted, and forgiven. Your name is written in the palms of my hands."

Answering God's Question

What is your name? As we have seen, God's question invites us to face up to ourselves. This is seldom easy. It usually takes a great deal of rigorous self-examination, a radical self-honesty, and much reflection on the way we have been living. Telling the truth about ourselves to God can be one of the hardest things we ever do. If it sounds too difficult, may I offer a simple word of encouragement. Becoming honest with ourselves and wrestling with these things with God opens our lives, like few other things can, to the incredible depths of God's grace and acceptance and power. We actually begin to experience in a deeper way our belovedness.

Here is one way for you to begin answering God's question:

Ask God to reveal the Jacob who lives in you. In other words, ask God to shed light on those times when you deliberately deceive those around you; times when you pretend to be someone that you are not; times when you try to evade the hard issues, rather than face up to them; times when you try to manipulate others to do what you want them to do. Telling God your name involves sharing the truth about things like these and being prepared to wrestle with God until you receive God's blessing.

Remember also that God wants to bless you. Do not be shy about asking God for this blessing. Make Jacob's prayer your own. "I will not let you go, unless you bless me." Try to be as open-ended as you can regarding the nature of God's blessing. We usually don't know what God's blessing is going to look like. Even though God is dependable and trustworthy, there is always a surprising unpredictability in the ways God deals with us. So, be expectant that God is going to bless you so that you can become a blessing to those around you.

Above all, hear the whisper of the Spirit within you, telling you that you are God's beloved. Try the prayer exercise outlined in the previous section. Come before the crucified Jesus in your imagination. Let the Cross demonstrate the depth and extent of God's personal love for you. See the light of God's love streaming toward you in the present moment. Claim your new name as the core truth of your existence. From your very beginnings you have been loved by God with the love of Jesus Christ which will never, ever let you go. Know this and live!

Questions for Small Groups

1. How do you feel about your name?
2. In what ways can you identify with Jacob?
3. What kind of inner change do you want God to bless you with?
4. What does it mean for you that your new name is "God's beloved"?

Chapter 5

What Are You Doing Here?

It was a scary moment. The other day I found myself stuck in a traffic jam on the busy highway into Johannesburg. Turning on the radio, I heard that a truck had overturned a few miles ahead. It would take at least a couple of hours to clear the road. To make matters worse, at that very moment a flickering dashboard light reminded me that my fuel was low. Since I could not exit the highway, the prospect of running out of gas suddenly became a very real and frightening possibility.

As it happened, it did not turn out that badly. Workers cleared the highway sooner than expected. I got off at the next off-ramp and found my way to a nearby filling station. It was a huge relief. As the attendant filled up my car's empty tank, I firmly resolved that I would never again allow myself to get into a similar predicament. Before setting out on any journey, even a short one into Johannesburg, I would make sure that I had enough gas. Sounds like common sense, I know, but it took this nerve-racking experience to drive the lesson home.

This experience serves as a helpful parable. As we drive on the highway of life, at times we are seriously at risk of running out of fuel. In other words, we sometimes live in such a way that we become vulnerable to exhaustion or the crisis of burn-out as some call it today. Thankfully, we have warning lights that come on when our emotional and spiritual reserves are dangerously low. If we can recognize them, these symptoms remind us to pay attention to the way we are living, to be aware of what is draining us, and to always ensure that our energy resources get regularly replenished.

What are these warning lights? There are many: We may have difficulty sleeping or lose interest in food. We may get constant headaches. We experience a chronic tiredness of the sort that is not helped by sleep or ordinary rest. We may struggle with gastrointestinal disturbances. We might frequently show uncharacteristic forms of behavior such as outbursts of anger or resentment or self-pity. Are any of these lights flashing at the moment for you? If they are, you may want to reflect with me on Elijah's experience of exhaustion and burnout and the question that came to him in the midst of his crisis.

You will find this part of Elijah's story in chapters 18 and 19 of the First Book of Kings. There you can read about a time in his life when everything came to a complete standstill and he ran away, deep into the desert. In a lonely cave on a mountain God asked him, "What are you doing here, Elijah?" (19:13). Interestingly, this crisis in Elijah's life, along with the question that God put to him, opened up for him a number of new opportunities. Let us explore his experience and see what we can learn from it. If you are in a similar state of exhaustion and burnout right now, Elijah's experience could lead you toward new opportunities for yourself as well.

An Opportunity to Stop

A few years ago I taught my two children how to drive. I can still remember our first lessons. On both occasions, as we got into the car, I said to each of them, "The first thing you need to know about this car is how to stop it." Certainly there are many more spectacular skills for a driver to develop than stopping the car, but few of them are more important than this basic skill. After all, picture a driver who proceeds along the highway with expertise and competence and speed but who cannot stop. Imagine what would happen. Eventually the driver would get so tired that he or she would fall asleep at the wheel and have a serious accident!

Exactly the same principle applies to our daily lives. As we drive along the highway of life, we need to develop many skills and competencies. We must learn how to communicate, how to get along with others, how to plan, how to delegate, how to strategize, how to raise our children, how to do our jobs effectively, and so on. Yet one basic skill underlies all these things: the art of learning how to stop. Unless we learn how to do this, we shall also eventually crash and burn out in one way or another.

Stopping gives us the time to renew our energy and to replenish our emotional and spiritual resources.

There are many good reasons to stop. Stopping gives us time to renew our energy and to replenish our emotional and spiritual resources. It gives us time when we can gather ourselves together, relax, and become calmer within. It's almost impossible to reflect thoughtfully on our lives when we are continually living at full speed. Before we realize it, we find ourselves operating on autopilot, going from one activity to another without much thought. In contrast, stopping for a while enables us to recognize more clearly those destructive patterns of living that push our lives beyond their God-given limits and then to make clear choices to live in a more healthy and life-giving way.

One of the few good things about experiencing exhaustion and burnout is that it forces us to stop. Certainly we can see this happening in Elijah's life in his time of crisis. When he took refuge in the cave, he experienced the benefit of stopping. He became quiet and could listen to what God was trying to say to him. His depleted energy levels started to be replenished. Most importantly, he was able to take a long hard look at the question that God asked him, "What are you doing here?" He was able to open up to God about those events and experiences that had brought his life to this point.

It may be a good idea to check and see whether you can stop before you end up in the same exhausted state as Elijah. You can do this right now, as I did while writing this chapter. Why don't you just stop and do nothing for the next five minutes? Sit quite still. Become aware of your breathing, and notice what is happening in your body. Sometimes the attempt to do this can be very revealing. We discover that we find it very difficult to sit still and be present to God and to ourselves. Remember, this is not a trivial matter at all. Learning to stop can save us from crashing!

An Opportunity to Listen to God

Once we have learned to stop we can begin listening. Elijah found this out the hard way. When he ran away and hid in the cave on Mount Horeb, he fortunately put himself in a position to hear God. Significantly, when God spoke to the exhausted prophet, it was not through the great wind or the violent earthquake or the blazing fire. Rather we read that the voice of the Lord came as a "gentle whisper" (1 Kings 19:12).

When Elijah heard it he realized he needed to focus on what God was trying to say to him. We read that he pulled his cloak over his face and went out and stood at the mouth of the cave and tried to listen. Then a quiet voice asked him, "What are you doing here, Elijah?"

God sometimes speaks so quietly that we have to move very close to hear the Divine Whisper.

Listening to God means getting closer so that we can hear the Divine Whisper. Recently I heard a story that illustrates this truth.[1] A young man was going through a difficult time. He did not know which way to turn, so he went to visit an old preacher for guidance. Pacing about the preacher's study, the young man ranted and raved about his problem. "I've begged God to say something to help me. Tell me, sir, why does God not answer?" The old preacher, who sat across the room, said something in reply, something so quiet that it was almost inaudible. The young man walked across the room. "What did you say?" he asked. The old man repeated himself but again spoke very quietly. So the young man moved even closer until he was leaning on the old man's chair. "Sorry," he said, "I still can't hear you." With their heads close together, the old preacher whispered once more, "God sometimes speaks so quietly that we have to move very close to hear the Divine Whisper." This time the young man heard and understood what the old man was trying to tell him.

Usually a time of burnout and exhaustion forces us to find the time and space to move closer to God. This is a good thing because, as Elijah's experience teaches us, God usually prefers to speak quietly in a gentle whisper. Nothing gets our attention more than a whisper does. God's still small voice means that we need to move much closer and to become much more still if we want to hear what God may be whispering to us. There is no better opportunity for us to slow down and to listen than when we are tired and worn-out.

You may be wondering how the Divine Whisper comes to us. God's whisperings usually come to us in the form of a distinctive thought. Thoughts influenced by God usually have a certain "feel" about them. They prompt us to do loving things rather than destructive things. They lead us in the direction of a more creative life. They invite us to take better care of ourselves. They do not accuse or condemn but often urge us toward a better and more positive approach. They draw us into a closer walk with God. Learning to discern the Divine Whisper in our thoughts can become one of the greatest adventures in life. But, like Elijah, we must stop and listen.

An Opportunity to Get God's Perspective

When we are exhausted and burned out, it is also easy to lose perspective. The consequences of this can be deadly. Negative thoughts and feelings begin to dominate us. Even though we may have done well in many areas of our lives, we start to see ourselves as failures, blinded to all the positive aspects of our lives. We lose our sense of worth and begin to wonder whether our lives serve any useful purpose. We begin to believe that we can do nothing to change our situation. Deep down we may even start to feel that God cannot use us any more. Sometimes we may even wish to take our own lives.

Elijah experienced many of these feelings and thoughts. When God asked, "What are you doing here, Elijah?" the prophet was looking at his life through very dark glasses. "'I have had enough, LORD,'" he said. "'Take my life; I am no better than my ancestors'" (1 Kings 19:4). Elijah felt that he had given his utmost, which had not been good enough. He believed he was now the only one left on God's side and that his former allies wanted to kill him. A deep sense of failure had permeated his thinking, draining him of energy and leaving him utterly depleted. Can you see the destructive effects of losing perspective?

We can choose to evaluate our lives by conventional human standards, or we can choose to see things God's way.

However, God saw Elijah from a different perspective. In the ensuing dialogue, God made it clear that God still had work for the prophet to do. Elijah had to return to Israel and recruit new leadership. From God's point of view Elijah's failures had not made him unfit for God's use. God also told Elijah that not everyone had lost faith; seven thousand people remained in Israel who had not bent their knees to the pagan god Baal. In effect, God was saying to Elijah something like, "What are you doing here, Elijah? See things from a new perspective. Your work has not been completed. I still have faith in you. I still want to use you."

In our moments of exhaustion and burnout, we have a choice to make. We can choose to evaluate our lives by conventional human standards, or we can choose to see things God's way. A few simple questions can help us determine the difference between these two perspectives. Does God call us to be successful or to be faithful? Is God more interested in quantity or in quality? Does God take a short-term or a long-term view? Is God more concerned about things or about people? When we view these questions in the light of God's conversation with Elijah, the answers are obvious. In each of them the second option is always God's perspective.

You may be able to identify with Elijah as he sat in the cave. Will you hear the question, "What are you doing here?" as a challenge to begin to see things from God's point of view? Some years ago I can remember doing this. A few people in whom I had invested a great deal of time, energy, and effort decided to leave the congregation where I served. Almost overnight I became overwhelmed by a sense of deep tiredness and failure. I found myself echoing Elijah's prayer, "I have had enough, Lord!" I took a day off to be alone with God. As I began to look through God's eyes at what had happened, the situation seemed a little less bleak. The next day I returned to my work with greater energy and more hope. May you also catch a glimpse of God's perspective on your current experience or circumstance.

Answering God's Question

"What are you doing here?" Assuming that you resonate with Elijah's experience, I invite you to tell God how you have come to be where you are at this moment. Events and experiences may have knocked you down or exhausted you. Disappointments and failures may have robbed you of energy. There may be "drivers" in your life that make it difficult for you to stop and be still.

Tell God about these things, and then be quiet and try to hear what God may be wanting to say to you through them.

The question also challenges us, as it did Elijah, to get God's broader perspective on what is happening in our lives. Remember that from God's point of view, certain things are more important than others. Faithfulness matters more than success, quality more than quantity, the long term more than the short term, people more than things.

As you look at your life through God's eyes, share with God those instances where you have allowed outside pressures and conventional human perspectives to shape your life more than God's perspective. What would it mean for you to change perspective in these areas?

In his paraphrase of the Bible called *The Message,* Eugene Peterson gives us a wonderful interpretation of Jesus' invitation in Matthew's Gospel to those who are exhausted and burned out. It goes like this.

> Are you tired? Worn out? Burned out on religion? Come to me. Get away with me and you'll recover your life. I'll show you how to take a real rest. Walk with me and work with me—watch how I do it. Learn the unforced rhythms of grace. I won't lay anything heavy or ill-fitting on you. Keep company with me and you'll learn to live freely and lightly (Matt. 11:28-30).

Here we find the real antidote to our weariness. Respond from your heart to this invitation, and discover the rest that God wants to give you as you travel on the highway of life.

Questions for Small Groups

1. When have you experienced exhaustion or the crisis of burnout? What was it like? What were your warning lights?
2. When do you take time to stop?
3. How does God speak to you? How do you know it is God who is speaking?
4. What would it mean for you to look at your present life from God's perspective?

Chapter 6

What Are You Looking For?

A few days before Christmas last year, I went to the nearby mall to buy some gifts. While waiting in the line to pay, a couple from my congregation walked by. They were both pushing baskets piled with items they had just bought. Thinking that they had finished shopping for the day, I said that they must be relieved to be going home. I still haven't forgotten their answer. "No," said the husband rather wearily, "we still haven't found what we are looking for."

The man's reply reminds me of our restless hearts. We are constantly looking for something, seeking something, wanting something. Something more, beyond ourselves, something we don't have at the moment. Something that will make us happier, give our lives more meaning, deepen our sense of significance. Seemingly we are always searching for something that will enable us to live fuller, happier, and freer lives. Sadly, our lives often resemble the couple I met in the mall. We walk up and down the aisles of life, pushing baskets overflowing with good things but still have not found what we really desire.

Significantly, Jesus' first question in the Gospels connects with this search. Picture briefly the background setting in which he asked the question. John the Baptizer was talking with two of his disciples. As they discussed together, Jesus walked by. John pointed toward him and called out, "Look, here is the Lamb of God" (NRSV). Intrigued by this description of the passing stranger, the two disciples began to follow Jesus. Suddenly Jesus stopped, turned around, and asked, "What are you looking for?" (John 1:38).

Imagine how this question must have floored these two characters. Here they are, obviously searching for something that is missing in their lives. Jesus asks them what they are looking for. His direct question has several layers of meaning. First of all, it urged the two disciples to listen to their hearts. It also challenged them to discover what they desired most. It especially invited them to ask for what they wanted. Without a doubt the question started them on an inner journey that would ultimately change their lives.

Notice one other aspect of this story. We learn the name of only one of the disciples who stood with John the Baptizer: Andrew, Simon Peter's brother. The other disciple is not named. Some scholars have suggested it might have been the Gospel writer himself. The lack of a name also suggests another option. Maybe, as Jean Vanier points out, it is to invite each one of us to identify with the unnamed disciple.[1] We may all respond to this question as if it were put to us personally. So let's explore what it means for our own lives today. It may just change us for the better, as it did those to whom Jesus first asked it.

Listening to Our Hearts

The first thing Jesus' question urges us to do is to listen to our own hearts. The word *heart* occurs over eight hundred times in the First Testament and does not refer to our physical heart. It is a metaphor that expresses the deep center of our lives, the core of our personalities, the person we really are. When we say that someone has shared his or her heart with us, it means that we have been given access to the most sacred and secret depths of who he or she is. When we listen to our hearts, therefore, we seek to pay close attention to our innermost yearnings and longings.

Yet we often avoid embarking on this inward quest. We make excuses: we don't have the time or we are too busy or we can't trust our hearts or it's a waste of time or we don't know how to go about it or it's too painful or it's too sentimental or we think our reasoning offers a better guide to life . . . the list goes on and on. Whatever excuse you and I may use, the result is always the same. We miss the opportunity to look into the deeper places of our hearts.

The consequences are very sad. I know this from my own experience and from listening for over thirty years to the inner longings of people's lives. When we are deaf to the cry of our own hearts, we cheat ourselves. We rob ourselves of living a life that is marked by depth and wonder and passion. We miss out on experiencing beautiful, intimate relationships with each other and with God. Instead we find ourselves living superficially—busy but going nowhere of any significance. Little wonder that, even in the midst of our outwardly successful and affluent lives, we sometimes hear ourselves saying, "I still haven't found what I am looking for."

Even in the midst of our outwardly successful and affluent lives, we sometimes hear ourselves saying, "I still haven't found what I am looking for."

Will you allow Jesus' question, "What are you looking for?" to lead you deeper into your heart? At first it may not be easy to find your way, especially if you have been living on the surface for a long while. To help you on this journey into the inner world of your desires and longings, you may need some help. Certainly you will need some silence and space. The simple exercise in the next section may help in the process, so keep reading! Whatever effort is required, be assured it will be worthwhile. Just ask those two seekers in the Gospel of John—Jesus' question completely changed the direction of their lives.

Discovering What We Desire Most

The second challenge this question poses is that we discover what we desire most. This is not as simple as it sounds. Just try answering this question for yourself right now. It's often difficult to respond clearly. Finding words to express our innermost longings does not come easily. Perhaps this is why the disciples themselves gave such a seemingly superficial answer when they were first asked what they wanted. Their immediate response was, "Rabbi . . . , where are you staying?"(John 1:38). Nonetheless Jesus took their response seriously and invited them to come and spend some time with him.

One reason we find it so hard to know
what we most desire is that we
have so many desires.

One reason we find it so hard to know what we most desire is that we have so many desires. Some are quite superficial, like, "I would really like a new car." Others are much deeper, sometimes coming from painful places within our hearts. I think of a childless couple longing for a baby, a single person wanting a partner, a sick person hoping to get well. Sometimes our desires may clash with one another. I can feel that conflict right now as I sit here trying to write this chapter. Part of me wants to write; another part of me would like to go outside, walk around the garden, and just chill out. It's not easy to know which desire to follow at this moment.

How then do we discover what we most deeply desire? Let me share an exercise that I find helpful.[2] Imagine that you have died and someone writes your eulogy for the funeral. The exercise is to write your own eulogy—not the one you are most likely to receive but what you would like people to say about you at your funeral. Let your imagination roam freely. You don't need to show what you write to anyone else. Just be sure to put down on paper what you really want said about you. In other words, be sure that your eulogy fulfills your deepest desires as you are aware of them in this moment.

I first did this exercise several years ago. I learned a number of things, but one stood out. Clearly, much of my everyday living can so easily become sidetracked by relatively superficial desires. To be more specific—and this is a confession—my whole attention can sometimes be dominated by concerns like how I come across to others, being liked by those around me, and trying to prove myself. These desires all seemed so stupid as I wrote them down on paper. None of these things was part of the obituary I wanted for myself. They did not reflect the deepest desires of my heart at all.

Take a few moments to consider the following questions. They are designed to get you thinking about the eulogy you would most like to have. Would you like to be remembered as someone who

- loved deeply or was always self-centered and selfish?
- was honest or was deceitful?
- was generous or was tightfisted?
- responded with compassion to those in need or never cared?
- loved life and cherished each moment or complained constantly?

Remember, these questions are not about how you are living at the moment; they are about what you desire most for your life.

Asking for What We Want

The third endeavor this question invites us to undertake is to ask for what we want. Those who take their journey with God seriously are sometimes surprised by this invitation. After all, are we not supposed to put aside what we want? Should we not rather try to find out what God wants us to do? Did not Jesus teach us to pray, "Your will be done on earth as it is in heaven"? What is the connection between our desires and God's will? Are these things not always in conflict with each other? These important questions deserve careful thought.

Here is an analogy to get us thinking.[3] Imagine a couple getting married. They have written their own vows for the wedding service. The groom says to his bride, "You are my heart's delight, and I love you with all of my being. However, you must understand that from this moment on, you must not expect me to have the slightest interest in your wants and desires. Henceforth, until death do us part, your happiness consists in your submitting yourself to my will with total dedication and with no thought for your own." How do you think the bride would respond? Not very well, I think.

Many people believe God is like this bridegroom. Yet our Gospel story reveals a very different picture of God. When Jesus asked the disciples what they were looking for, his question demonstrated once and for all that God is concerned and interested in our desires. Clearly God does not want us to ignore our longings, push them aside, or put them to death. Indeed, the exact opposite is true. God wants us to listen to the desires of our hearts, to befriend them, to understand them, and then to ask for what we want. Whatever our longings may be, God really is interested. What a contrasting image of God this is from the one provided by the demanding bridegroom above!

Whatever our longings may be,
God really is interested.

This does not mean that God will simply give us what we ask for. Not all our desires express the true longings of our hearts. Some of them are selfish and quite superficial. If God were to grant them, we would never discover the deeper ones underneath. Other desires sometimes push us in destructive directions. If given expression, they could cause great pain. Nonetheless, we need to bring all of them into the open before God. Only then can God give us the light we need to sort out the healthy from the unhealthy.

Over the past few years I have been learning a little more about the crucial difference between our healthy and unhealthy desires. Unhealthy desires make our world smaller. They isolate us from other people and pull us away from God. They seek to enslave us by tempting us into destructive attachments. On the other hand, healthy desires expand our world. They connect us with others in life-giving ways and draw us toward God. They invite us to share God's dream for the world. Most significantly, when we follow them we experience ourselves coming alive in new and exciting ways. We come alive to ourselves, in our relationships, and to God's presence in and around us.

Answering God's Question

What are you looking for? Clearly Jesus was aware of the powerful role that our desires play in our lives. Think about it for a moment. Our desires shape who we become. They give us energy to pursue our dreams, our goals. They influence our decisions. Sometimes we may even allow our will to become enslaved to a desire. Should this happen, and the desire is an evil one, the results can be tragic. Doubtless our desires can give us life or destroy us. Little wonder that Jesus invites us to listen to our hearts, discover what our desires really are, and bring them into the light of God's presence.

A good way to begin this listening is to take some uninterrupted time with God to reflect on your desires. What do you most want? What are you looking for in the years remaining to you? What do you still want to do with your life? What kind of person do you want to become before you die? What kind of life do you want to live? Please do not come to conclusions about your answers too quickly. Sometimes the way to get in touch with our deeper longings is to start with the superficial ones and try to discern what lies beneath and beyond them.

Share your reflections with God, and ask God to help you to sift through them. It helps to write them down on a piece of paper. Do not try to sort them out with your own cleverness and understanding. Sometimes it's hard for us to distinguish the weeds from the wheat. Simply be honest. Rather say something like this to God, "Lord, here are my real longings. Please show me those that reflect your heart and those that don't. Help me to turn from destructive desires, and give me the courage to follow those that will genuinely bring me alive." Over time you will experience God giving you the light you need to do the work of discernment.

Psalm 37:4 reminds us that God grants the desires of our hearts—not the superficial ones that shout for instant gratification or the destructive ones that keep us in bondage or the evil ones that allow us to use people for our own selfish ends but those that come from the deepest place of who we are. These are the God-prompted ones, the ones that God initiates in our hearts, the ones that reflect God's will for our lives. When we follow these, they draw us toward an abundance of life. May the Spirit of God lead us to these life-giving longings.

Questions for Small Groups

1. On a line where 1 indicates "deeply restless" and 10 indicates "utterly content," where would you place yourself at the moment?
2. How would you like to be remembered at your funeral?
3. How do you work out the difference between healthy and unhealthy desires in your life?
4. What are you looking for today?

Chapter 7

Who Do You Say I Am?

Have you ever read through one of the Gospels in one sitting? It is something well worth doing. There are some huge benefits. You get to know Jesus better. You see more clearly how his life unfolded through its different phases. You develop a deeper understanding of what he taught and what he stood for. You notice how often he took time to be with his Father, especially at key moments in his life. In a nutshell, you notice things about Jesus and the Gospel story that are easily missed when you only read a few verses at a time. Let me give you one example.

If you sit down and read straight through Mark's Gospel, one thing stands out almost immediately: the Gospel clearly divides into two halves. Of the sixteen chapters, the first eight are full of life; they pulsate with energetic action. Jesus moves from village to village—sharing the good news of God's availability, freeing those imprisoned in the grip of evil, healing the sick, feeding the hungry, stilling storms and seas, telling parables and having a really fruitful time of ministry.

Then midway through the eighth chapter, the mood changes. You can almost feel it. It becomes much more tense and urgent; a sense of danger fills the air. Jesus begins to talk about suffering and tells his disciples that following him will not be easy. He repeatedly emphasizes that he is going to die but will rise again. One biblical scholar, reflecting on this abrupt shift in the atmosphere of the Gospel, states, "The last eight chapters of the Gospel are dominated by death talk."[1] The contrast is striking.

This turning point revolves around a question asked by Jesus. He had taken his disciples to Caesarea Philippi, a region north of the land of Israel, on the slopes of Mount Hermon, by the source of the river Jordan. It would seem that he wanted to be alone with them, away from the crowds. He needed to talk with them about a potentially explosive matter. Who did they, his closest companions, think he was. They had witnessed his miracles, listened to his teachings, experienced his companionship. But what did they believe about him? This was the burning issue: "Who do you say I am?" (Mark 8:29).

This question strikes a relevant chord. We live in a day and age that is fascinated by the figure of Jesus. More books have been written about him in the past thirty years than in all the centuries before. Movies like *The Passion of the Christ* become box office hits. Scholars hotly debate the authenticity of his words and actions as recorded in the four Gospels. Even those who say they want nothing to do with him use his name when they curse! It's hard to remain neutral about him. Small wonder that our response to the question "Who do you say that I am?" shapes our lives more than our answer to any other question. Let us take some time to wrestle with it ourselves.

Keeping Company with Jesus in the Gospels

The four Gospels are the best place to begin exploring who Jesus is. Without them it would be nearly impossible for us to know anything about him. Almost every line of these books has the power to lead us into greater knowledge of the person of Jesus. Knowing this to be true, spiritual guides throughout the centuries have encouraged serious seekers to meditate constantly on the figure of Jesus as revealed in the Gospels. I have sought to take this ancient counsel seriously. Often I will encourage those who want to know more about Jesus with one sentence: "Keep company with Jesus in the Gospels."

Should you want to do this, here is a simple exercise. Set some time aside, an hour or so, to read through a Gospel at one sitting. It can be helpful to do this more than once over a period of time. As you read, keep company with Jesus. Catch a glimpse of his relationship with God whom he called "*Abba* Father." Witness the deep intimacy and closeness between him and the Father. Notice the way he relates to people, especially those who live on the fringes of his society—the tax collectors, the prostitutes, the lepers, and so on. Listen to the words he speaks and the message he brings. Explore the way he sees the world. Watch what he does and the manner in which he does it. How do you respond to him?

For about thirty years, I have been seeking to do this. During this time I have wrestled with the question: "Who do you say that I am?" I have come to see Jesus as the most alive, aware, and responsive human being who has ever lived. I have come to recognize his dying as revealing love's response in the face of evil. I have come to realize that something extraordinary must have taken place after the crucifixion that transformed those frightened and grieving disciples into bold witnesses willing to die for their beliefs. I have found it most reasonable to accept the explanation the Bible gives for this transformation: That this man Jesus was fully human, one of us, and yet at the same time one who is God come in the flesh. Or stated simply, I have come to believe that he is *the* One.

I have come to see Jesus as the most alive,
aware, and responsive human being
who has ever lived.

You may struggle with my rather exclusive assertion about who Jesus is. "Surely," I hear you say, "there are other spiritual teachers who are equally worth following." When I am challenged like this, I usually respond with a story told to me by Dallas Willard, one of the leading thinkers in the world of philosophy today. A doctoral student at a prestigious American university asked him, "Professor, why do you, an intelligent, thoughtful, and well-educated man, follow Jesus?" With characteristic simplicity Dallas responded with a question of his own. "Tell me," he asked the inquiring student, "who else do you have in mind?"[2]

Dallas was not being flippant; he was saying, "Tell me who you believe in, and let us make an honest comparison. If what you believe in is better than what I have come to understand in Jesus, I am prepared to change my thinking." The point is that when we come to know Jesus deeply, we will find that he is the best choice when compared to all the others. I have looked at other teachers and other ways; even though they have much to offer, they fall short of what I have found in Jesus in so many crucial respects. I am very clear in my experience about who Jesus is for me. He is the best and the greatest. He is *the* One.

Developing a Personal Knowledge of Jesus

Keeping company with Jesus in the Gospels is one essential component in coming to know who he is. But it needs to be balanced with another kind of knowing. As we read the Gospels over and over, we learn about Jesus. We are introduced to his words and actions. We are told about his death and his resurrection. We build up what could be called a historical knowledge. Yet we may still miss knowing who Jesus really is. We need another kind of knowledge as well—a personal knowledge of who he is from our own experience of him. Both these kinds of knowledge are important when it comes to getting to know the person of Jesus.

A simple illustration may help here. I have been married to Debbie for almost thirty years. Many people in our community know about her. They have a certain historical knowledge of her. They know what she looks like, where she teaches, the kind of clothes she wears, the way she does her hair, and some other external things. But they do not know her as intimately as I know her. They have not experienced the depth of her love, the extent of her forgiveness, her ruthless honesty, her confidence in God, as I have. These qualities have been revealed to me through my relationship with her. They make up my "personal" knowledge of her, a precious gift that has been given me as I have come to know her over a length of time. This kind of knowledge goes much deeper than historical knowledge.

Similarly, when it comes to getting to know Jesus, we need both these kinds of knowing—the historical and the personal. Both are essential. The first is a knowledge about Jesus that comes mainly from our immersion in the Gospel stories. The second is a deeper knowledge that comes when we give ourselves to him and begin to follow him. We will not come to know who Jesus really is without bringing these two ways of knowing together. This process does not happen overnight. Like getting to know another human being intimately, it will take a lifetime and perhaps even longer.

As he did two thousand years ago,
Jesus still calls us to be his disciples.

Can you see now why Christianity involves a radical giving of ourselves to Jesus? As he did two thousand years ago, Jesus still calls us to be his disciples. He invites us to say today, "Lord Jesus, I have read about you in the Gospels. I have come to recognize something very special about you, something very special about the way you died and how you live beyond death today. Now I want to bring the story about you in the Gospels together with the story of my life. I want to get to know you personally within the particulars of my own experience and relationships and community. And so I give myself unconditionally to you."

You may struggle to give yourself like this. Do not force yourself beyond what you are able to give. Know that you are not alone in this. It is difficult enough to give oneself completely to someone we see, let alone to someone we cannot see. Genuine surrender seldom happens quickly or without a battle. Usually it happens gradually, one day at a time, as we learn to trust the love of Christ that we have seen in the Gospels. Difficult as trusting ourselves to Christ may be, it is only within such a personal relationship that we will come to know in our own experience who he really is. Are you willing to embark on this journey of surrender and trust?

Experiencing Jesus as Our Personal Companion

Something else happens when we give ourselves to Jesus. In the power of his Spirit, he steps out from the pages of the Gospels. He becomes our personal companion. Amazingly, we begin to discover how he can be our living friend today, just as he was for those who left their nets and followed him by the Sea of Galilee. As we walk with him, together with others, he shows us his way for our lives and gives us the power to walk in it as well. We learn that his yoke is easy and his burden light. Most wonderful of all, we discover that we are never alone, no matter what we are going through.

Millions of people from various backgrounds can testify to this reality. One testimony that has touched me is that of Joseph Girzone. Let me tell you a little about him. A number of years ago he had to retire from the Catholic priesthood because of his health. He chose not to accept any compensation from his church, even though he had no income. For the first time in his life he was nearly penniless. He had just enough to survive. He had no money for clothes. He made his furniture from some boards that he had bought cheaply. He knew for the first time in his life what it was to be genuinely poor in the world's sense of the word. He also began to practice what Jesus taught in a way that he had never done before.

In his autobiography *Never Alone* Girzone tells of one particular experience. He was taking a walk and wondering what he would do for supper, because he had no money. Walking along the side of the road, he thought he saw some money in the ditch. He wondered how such money could have gotten there when it was so far from anywhere. He took a closer look, bent down, and sure enough, lying in the ditch, neatly folded, was just enough money for supper. In that moment he could almost hear Jesus saying to him, "I told you not to worry, I would take care of you."

Sometime later, Girzone's life situation changed completely. He began to write novels about a person called Joshua, his way of introducing people to Jesus and his message. Millions of Girzone's books have been sold around the world. Money has now become a painful burden in his life. Trying to use it wisely has not been easy. In *Never Alone* he writes a dedication to Jesus at the beginning of the book. It describes beautifully how we can come to know Jesus as our personal companion when we entrust ourselves fully to him. Here is his dedication:

> I dedicate this book to my friend who is always by my side and in my heart, who is never far when I am lonely and confused, who always gives peace to my soul when I am troubled and frightened, and fearful of the future. I share with him my deepest secrets, my joy, my sorrow, my accomplishments, my shame. He always understands. He never accuses or criticizes, but often suggests a different way of doing things. When he does he inevitably prepares the way so it is not as impossible as I thought it might be.

> Over the years I have learned to trust him. It was not easy. I thought that in following him I would have to give up all the fun in my life, but I found that he is the source of all joy and adventure, and, indeed, he turned my life into a great adventure at a time when I thought it was about to come to an end. I would like to suggest that he could become your friend too, if you would like him to be. Do not be afraid! He will respect your freedom and your independence more than anyone you have ever met, because he created you to be free. He just wants more than anything that you will accept him as your friend. If you do, I can promise you, you will never be alone.[3]

Answering God's Question

Who do you say that I am? Jesus' question echoes down the corridors of history into the present moment. Now it is time for you to explore your own response.

Who is Jesus Christ for you? Is he a myth created by the clever imaginations of the Gospel writers? a great human teacher and prophet? a healer who was able to do great miracles once upon a time? some sort of Superman figure, able to swoop down and rescue you from all your difficulties? Or is he Someone else, Someone more, Someone who is totally and fully human, and yet who all the time is also God revealing God's self to us? How do you respond?

As we have already seen, the best way to begin exploring these questions lies in reading the Gospels. Take some time to do the Gospel reading exercise described earlier. Ask God to help you see Jesus more fully as he really is. Ask also to see him, not only as he is in the Gospels but also as he has lived throughout history in the lives of his followers and throughout the universe. Often we can catch glimpses of his beauty and greatness in those who have given themselves to him.

Alongside these explorations, it will be important to engage personally with Jesus. Getting to know him is far more than just a head thing. It's also about giving yourself deeply to the One whom you want to get to know. Remember, there are two kinds of knowing. There is simply no way you will come to know Jesus without entrusting as much as you can of yourself to as much as you know of him. This risky step involves the simple faith that Jesus is alive and present with us right now and wants to make himself known to all who truly seek him. What do you think and feel about taking this step? Share these thoughts and feelings with God.

As always, the important thing is to be completely honest. Our understanding of Jesus usually develops and deepens over time. When Peter answered Jesus' question and said to him, "You are the Messiah," he was still on a journey toward knowing who Jesus really was. Calling Jesus Messiah at this point in Mark's

Gospel did not mean that Peter was calling him "divine" or "the second person of the Trinity" or "God." That fuller understanding of Jesus' identity would only come later for Peter. Similarly, as we wrestle with this question, we may also find that it will take some time before we fall on our knees at the feet of Jesus and cry out, "You are my Lord and my God."

This question and Peter's answer marked a turning point in Mark's Gospel. May your response become the turning point in your own life.

Questions for Small Groups

1. What is the most interesting item you have learned about Jesus recently?
2. How has this recent learning affected your life and relationships?
3. In what way do you most struggle with Jesus and his message?
4. How would you today, using your own language, respond to Jesus' question, "Who do you say I am?"

We need to be willing to go on a journey of change, risk, and obedience.

If you feel paralyzed like this little bird, there is some wonderful good news in the Bible. God wants to free you and me. However, an important precondition accompanies this freedom. We need to be willing to embark on a journey of change, risk, and obedience. This is the message of that healing story in the fifth chapter of John's Gospel. One sabbath day, Jesus came to the pool of Bethesda in Jerusalem. Those who were sick, blind, and lame gathered there in hopes of a miraculous healing. Jesus noticed a paralyzed man who had been lying there for thirty-eight years. But instead of healing him immediately, as he had done with so many others, Jesus asked him the question, "Do you want to get well?"

This is the same question God asks us when we find ourselves paralyzed in one way or another. Do we really want to be well? It is an unexpected, provocative, and challenging question. It catches our attention right away. Do we really want to live beyond paralysis? Before we answer too quickly, let us look at some of its possible meanings.

A New Freedom

First of all, the question points us toward the freedom that Jesus offers. When Jesus asked the paralytic if he wanted to get well, he was in effect saying to him, "I want to offer you a freedom beyond your paralysis, a freedom that this world cannot give you. A freedom that can bring you release from all the things that hold you captive. A freedom that bursts with new possibilities and potential for living. It's a freedom that comes from God, and only I can give it to you."

You may be wondering how I can assume that Jesus was saying all this when he asked that simple question. Here is the basis of my assumption. The pool of Bethesda was a well-known healing place. It was situated in Jerusalem, just north of the Temple. The pool still exists, and if you go to Jerusalem you can see it for yourself. Also, as New Testament historian Tom Wright points out, it wasn't just a Jewish healing place. The evidence suggests that many non-Jews also regarded it as a healing shrine. At one stage it was dedicated to Asclepius, worshiped throughout the ancient Mediterranean world as a god of healing.[2]

The people believed that whenever the waters were stirred, the first person to get into the pool would be healed. So each day the sick would sit there, waiting. However, the shrine was not that successful in practice. The pool of Bethesda spoke of the possibilities of a new freedom but failed to deliver on its promise. Years would go by without those sitting there experiencing the liberation their hearts longed for.

[Jesus'] question, "Do you want to get well?" brings with it the hope that we can live beyond paralysis, the hope that we can be set free from whatever holds us captive.

A similar thing happens today. Think about all the promises of freedom that our world offers: self-help books, television programs, self-appointed gurus, New Age philosophies, political theories, and the like. However, they don't seem to be working too well. In spite of the tidal flood of promised "freedoms," ever-increasing numbers of people live in bondage to fear, depression, despair, addiction, meaninglessness, and what seems to be a tragic inability to get along with those they say they love most.

Wonderfully, along comes Jesus sent by God to make available a new freedom to all—to live, to love, and to serve. Today, in the power of his risen presence he continues to come to those of us who are paralyzed in our different ways. His question, "Do you want to get well?" brings with it the hope that we can live beyond paralysis. The hope that we can be set free from whatever holds us captive. The hope that we can fly again. The hope that we will find our voice and sing once more.

The Challenge of Change

Second, the question confronts us with the challenge of change. Certainly that is what it would have meant for the paralytic. Was he really willing to let go of his old way of life? Or had he become so accustomed to some of the benefits of being paralyzed that he really didn't want things to change? After all, he had people, friends, or relatives, who fetched and carried for him; people who fed him and took care of him. He didn't have to take responsibility for his life; others had to do that for him. Perhaps he felt a certain amount of comfort with his situation. To be healed would mean having to get up and take hold of life again.

Clearly Jesus wanted to know where he stood on this issue. Did he want to get well—or did he prefer to remain sick? If he wanted to make the shift from a life of paralysis into the radically new freedom that Jesus was offering him, he had to be willing to make the necessary changes.

The paralytic's initial response indicates a large degree of resistance. One would have expected a clear and definite yes. However, there was no positive response at all. In fact he avoided the question. He preferred to make a list of excuses for the situation that he was in. "Sir," the invalid replied, "I have no one to help me into the pool when the water is stirred. While I am trying to get in, someone else steps down ahead of me." These words suggest that he was trying to shift the blame to others for his predicament. It was their fault because they had not given him the help he needed.

There are some striking parallels between the paralytic and ourselves. Like him, we also sometimes avoid changing those aspects that would help us to live more freely. We prefer the attention and sympathy that we get from talking about our struggles. We also battle to let go of old patterns of destructive behavior in order to move into healthier ways of relating. We don't really want to take responsibility for living life fully again. We also sometimes play the "blame game" rather than take responsibility for the mess we are in. These are just a few of the ways that we, like the paralytic, resist the challenge of change.

I think of one painful example from my own marriage. For many years, when things did not go my way, I would play the "withdrawal game" with Debbie. I would withhold my attention, my affection, and sometimes even my presence. When she asked what was wrong I would usually blame her for the struggles we were having. This scenario would replay itself over and over again like a stuck record with a bad tune. Its effects on our relationship were paralyzing. We would become stuck in unexpressed anger, resentment, and sadness. A new freedom only began to break through when I was willing to stop this pattern of behavior, take responsibility, and face the challenge of change.

Today God asks you, "Do you want to get well?" How are you going to respond?

Perhaps you are feeling paralyzed in some way right now. Today God asks you, "Do you want to get well?" How are you going to respond? Are you willing to let go of some behavior or character defect in order to embrace the new thing that God wants to do in your life? Are you willing to stop blaming others and take responsibility for the person you want to become? In a nutshell, are you willing to confront the challenge of change? Without a decisive and positive response to this question, you cannot experience the freedom that Jesus wants to give.

The Risk of Obedience

Third, the question points to the risk of obedience. Take another look at the story. Despite the paralytic's initial resistance toward the challenge of change, Jesus yearned to liberate him. This becomes obvious when you follow the dialogue between the two of them. Immediately after Jesus had asked the paralytic whether he wanted to be well, he gave him the direct command, "Get up! Pick up your mat and walk." Notice how this instruction was specifically aimed at encouraging the paralytic to live more freely and fully beyond his paralysis.

The paralytic immediately obeyed Jesus' command. It must have taken immense courage and faith. Imagine some of his thoughts when Jesus told him to get up. *What happens if I fall? How will I cope not begging for a living? Can I trust this man's word? Will he help me if I obey?* Whatever he may have been thinking, the paralytic did what he was told to do. He picked up his mat, and he walked. Consider what would have happened if he had not taken this risk of obedience. Most probably, he would have come to the end of his life still sitting beside the pool, still paralyzed.

God begins to work miracles when we take a step of risky obedience.

This story's lesson is clear: God begins to work miracles when we take a step of risky obedience. A careful study of some of the other miracles in the Bible reinforces this truth. You see, miracles seldom happen out of the blue. They do not take place in the lives of those who are passive and do nothing. They are usually a mixture of God's loving power *and* our willingness to do whatever God asks us to do. Or to put it more personally in terms of the theme of this chapter, if you and I want to experience a new freedom, we need to reflect on what step God may be asking us to take in the midst of our paralysis. This step will be different but always deeply personal for each one of us.

Let me return to the story of my marriage. I clearly recall God's word to me in the midst of the struggle that I described earlier. It went something like this. "Trevor, don't cut yourself off from Debbie when you are unhappy. Rather share with her how you are feeling without accusing her or blaming her. My inner power will help you as you do this." As I put into practice this straightforward command from God, I did experience God's liberating power. Obviously I have needed to take this step again and again. But each time God has met me with a strength that comes from way beyond myself.

I would not dare presume what God might be saying to you in the midst of your own paralysis. But I do have a hunch that you will know. God's word to us is usually directly related to the situation in which we find ourselves. Usually, it comes as a thought that suggests a creative and life-giving way of moving forward. And it will always point toward the possibilities of a new freedom in your life and relationships. It could be that right now God is saying something like this to you:

- Find someone with whom you can share honestly the struggle you are having at this moment.
- Ask someone to pray with you that you may have a greater experience of God's power.
- Let go of the bitterness you are carrying, and begin the journey toward forgiveness.
- Say you are sorry.
- Reach out and touch your spouse.
- Walk away from the abusive situation you are in.
- Break the silence, and tell someone about the abuse you suffered as a child.

The list of possible examples is endless. The important thing is to do whatever it is that God is saying to us. Miracles seldom happen without taking the risk of obedience.

Answering God's Question

Do you want to get well? Do you really want to be free to live and love more deeply? Are you wanting to be released from those blockages that stop God's love from flowing through you? Do you want to be set free from the bondages in your life? Do you want to become free enough to carry out your little piece of God's dream for the mending of our broken world? God wants to free you for these possibilities, but you need to be willing to get up and to begin to walk again.

As we have already seen, you would think that the answer to this question would be quite obvious. However, this is not the case. There is always a cost in the journey toward freedom. There are some things that you may need to give up. There are destructive patterns of behavior from which you may need to turn away. There are some difficult situations for which you may need to take responsibility. Take some time to share with God your thoughts and feelings about these possible changes. Seek to be as honest and open as you can in your communication with God about these things.

Once you have spoken with God, take some time to listen to what God may be saying to you, especially with regard to that area of life in which you feel paralyzed. What risk of obedience does God want you to take? You may want to remember that God's word often takes the shape of a certain kind of thought. This thought usually sheds light on the next step on your path toward freedom. Take some time to write down what you think God may be saying to you, and speak to God about it.

May Jesus' question "Do you want to get well?" stir the breeze in your life, so that the bird may fly.

Questions for Small Groups

1. Describe one freedom that God has brought into your life and relationships.
2. How did this gift of freedom come to you?
3. Where do you experience "paralysis" (or "stuckness") at the moment?
4. What do you sense the risen Christ may be saying to you with regard to this particular paralysis?

Chapter 9

Why Are You Crying?

Over the past few years I have noticed that tears come much more easily to me than they used to. There could be a number of reasons for this. It may have something to do with getting older. Maybe, as the years go by, I am becoming more vulnerable. Or they may be linked to some past sadness that I have not fully dealt with. One of my favorite authors suggests that as we move through our fifties previously unexpressed sides of our personality sometimes begin to show themselves.[1] Perhaps, my recent tearfulness is linked to some hidden grief or pain that I have not worked through.

My tears come at different times and in different ways. Sometimes they come during a movie, like they did when I watched the heart-wrenching ending to *Tsotsi,* a locally produced film that won an Oscar in the best foreign language film category. Sometimes they come after doing a funeral, especially when I have just buried someone who has been killed tragically. Sometimes they come when I remember my mom and dad and think about all the sacrifices they made for me. Sometimes they come when I am faced with my failure to love deeply and unconditionally those closest to me. Recently they came when I received a letter from a friend who is physically disabled. She longs desperately for an intimate relationship but often finds herself rejected and ignored.

I share all these examples for a special reason: I would like to help you become more aware of the tears in your own life. Perhaps you also find your tears flowing more freely as you get older. Or maybe they are hidden away in a secret room of your heart. Whether they roll down your cheeks or remain bottled up inside, your tears may reflect any number of things. They may indicate the grief over the death of a dearly loved person, the breakup of a special relationship, the betrayal of a close friend, a deep disappointment, the loss of a business venture, or they may point toward a deep unmet longing that is sometimes too painful for you to name. The list goes on.

The good news is that our tears do not always have to end in sadness. They can lead us toward healing and growth and new beginnings.

The good news is that our tears do not always have to end in sadness. They can lead us toward healing and growth and new beginnings. They can open our eyes to angelic presences, human and divine, all around us. They can make our hearts more receptive to a deeper experience of God. They can become the means by which our whole lives are profoundly transformed. This is our discovery when we engage the question that the risen Jesus put to Mary Magdalene on that first Easter Sunday morning. He asked her, "Woman, why are you crying?" (John 20:15).

Recall for a moment the setting in which Jesus asks this question. Mary was weeping outside the tomb where Jesus had been buried. His body, which she had come to anoint, was gone. Imagine the depth of her anguish and confusion. Not only had her Lord and Master been crucified, but someone had now stolen his body. Then suddenly the question came, first from the angels inside the tomb and then from the risen Jesus standing behind her. It was a question that began a new journey for Mary, both into and through her pain. I want to suggest that if we are willing to grapple with this same question, something similar can happen for us.

Tears Are Okay

Jesus' question to Mary reminds us that tears are okay. Tears reflect the fact that we are vulnerable, fallible, and fragile human beings. Jesus knew this only too well. In his Sermon on the Mount he pronounced a special blessing on those who mourn. He himself was no stranger to tears. When he saw the grief of Mary and Martha for their brother Lazarus, he also wept (see John 11:35). Not surprisingly, therefore, when he found Mary crying outside the tomb, he did not condemn her. He did not say to her, "Come on, Mary, put a stop to your tears. Can't you see it's Easter Sunday morning? Cheer up and be strong now." Rather, he accepted her tears and reached out to her in her need.

Many of us, especially men, feel uncomfortable with our tears. Deep down we regard them as a sign of weakness. We try to keep them hidden, even when our hearts are breaking. I cannot count the number of times I have been with persons in tears, either when a loved one has died or after a funeral or during a counseling session, and they have said to me something like, "I am sorry for crying. I really must try to pull myself together."

There could be an even deeper reason for our struggle with tears. I became conscious of this aspect only recently. Together with my son I had gone to watch the film *Tsotsi.* During the movie we became aware of people laughing during some of the most painful scenes. People laughed when the gangster character robbed and then killed a train commuter. They laughed when he harassed a paraplegic beggar at the train station. They laughed when he stole the baby. They laughed when flies smothered the baby's face. Afterward, both my son and I were puzzled about why the audience had laughed during these sad moments.

Strangely, a few days later, I came across an article in a Johannesburg newspaper about the movie. Written by Justice Malala, the article focused on the same question my son and I had struggled with. Movingly, Justice wrote about the violence that had always been part of his growing up in South Africa. Reflecting on the scenes where one would have expected tears, he suggested that the laughter reflected the unhealed trauma of a nation that had gone crazy with violence. He wrote: "It has made me realize that all these people were not simply laughing. They have forgotten how to cry."[2]

Our tears put us in touch with our pain.
They help us to know where we are hurting.

Perhaps, for some deep reason, your heart has become so hardened that you have also forgotten how to cry. I pray that Jesus' question will help you to remember. Learning to cry again could bring about the beginning of a new journey toward wholeness, just like it did for Mary. Our tears put us in touch with our pain. They help us to know where we are hurting.

But you may now be asking, "So what can we do with our tears? If we indulge them, we may be guilty of self-pity. If we hide them, we run the risk of blocking our healing. Where do we go with them?" Jesus' question helps us to take another step.

Facing the Story Behind Our Tears

Jesus' question invites us to face the story behind our tears. Certainly this is what he invited Mary Magdalene to do. He was asking her to examine her pain, to put words to her sorrow, to allow her tears to find their voice. Mary had just disclosed to the angels the cause of her grief, "They have taken my Lord away and I don't know where they have put him." At that point, Jesus asked her, "Why are you crying?" Even though Mary does not recognize Jesus, she responds to his question by expressing her anguish at not finding his body.

Like Mary, we also need to respond to this question. We can do so in one of two ways. On the one hand, we can find someone with whom we feel safe enough to entrust our tears, someone who can be our "wailing wall." I will always be grateful for those special people who have come alongside me in my pain, listened without judgment, and held what I have shared in sacred trust. These people have included a caring psychiatrist, several dear friends, and most especially those closest to me. Each of them, at different times and in different ways, has been that wailing wall against which I could shed my tears.

On the other hand, we can also share our tears with God. Many of the psalms in the Bible teach us to do this. They show us how to talk simply and honestly to God about the deep groanings of our hearts and lives. We need to tell God about it. The psalmist repeatedly encourages us to speak aloud to God about our painful experiences. Think for a moment of some of the sentences we come across when we read the Psalms.

Sentences like, "To the LORD I cry aloud"; "Hear my prayer, O LORD, listen to my cry for help"; "How long, O LORD?"

Something healing and life-giving happens when we share our tears not just with God but also with another human being. Almost always when we take this step, we experience great relief and release. When we have the courage to do this, we do not feel so alone any more. We feel closer to one another as we become more open to sharing our struggles rather than boasting of our successes. Even more importantly, this sharing can lead us to find a new intimacy in our relationship with God. When we bring our tears to God in the presence of another person, there seems to be a response from God that helps us know that we are not alone. Sometimes we may even begin to sense that God shares our broken heart and weeps with us in our pain.

Something healing and life-giving happens when we share our tears not just with God but also with another human being.

One memory comes to mind immediately. I was leading a forty-eight-hour silent retreat for first-time retreatants. Halfway through the weekend a woman, whose nineteen-year-old son had been killed in a car accident, shared her tears with me. Her pain was immeasurable. I listened in respectful silence, hoping inwardly that I could be a wailing wall for her. A few hours later, upon entering the darkened chapel, I saw her kneeling before a stark crucifix; tears were streaming down her cheeks. She turned and said to me, "I can face tomorrow. I know God knows and suffers with me." Sharing her tears with God and another human being had made it possible for her to grieve with hope.

Moving from Tears to New Beginnings

Jesus' question helps us move from our tears to new beginnings. Notice how cleverly John communicates this good news. He tells us that Mary at first did not recognize Jesus. She thought he was the gardener. When we explore this garden image a little more, we catch fresh glimpses of the newness that God wants to give us on the other side of our tears. So let us dig a little deeper and try to see what may have been going on in the Gospel writer's mind when he tells us about Mary's perception of Jesus as the gardener.

Here is a question that may help with our digging. Where is the first mention of a garden in the Bible? I am sure that you know the answer: Genesis, where God created the first people and gave them responsibility to care for the garden where they had been placed. However, as you may also remember, things went radically wrong. They chose to live their own way instead of the way God wanted them to live. As a result, they lost their place in the garden. Tearful things like shame, sorrow, and separation entered their lives. Paradise was lost, and our early ancestors found themselves living outside the garden that was meant to be their home.

Now, as we move back to the Gospel story, keep this Genesis picture in the back of your mind. Can you see the strong links between the two? Both stories took place within a garden. Adam was called to care for the garden, while Mary mistook Jesus for a gardener. As one writer has suggested, "John wants us to see a connection between the garden of Eden and Jesus rising from the dead in a garden. There is a new Adam on the scene, and he is reversing the curse of death by conquering it. . . . And he's doing it in a garden."[3] In other words, this garden imagery is a powerful reminder that when Jesus met Mary in her tears, he wanted to bring her the resurrection gift of starting over again.

In the midst of our tears [the risen Christ] wants to help us to begin again, to experience new life and resurrection power.

This is what the risen Christ also wants to do for us. In the midst of our tears he wants to help us to begin again, to experience new life and resurrection power. As he did in Mary's life, he comes searching for us in our pain, calling us by name, and inviting us into a deeper intimacy. We do not always recognize him at first. Sometimes he comes to us through a caring friend, sometimes in the beauty of a sunset, sometimes in the bread and cup of a Communion service. Sometimes he comes in other unexpected and surprising ways. In whatever way we may experience his resurrection love and power, when we do, it always helps us to take another step through our suffering.

As you engage Jesus' question for yourself, allow this garden image to fill your heart and mind. It speaks of new creation, new growth, new possibilities. Jesus is the new Adam, alive and present throughout the universe, who is making all things new. He is the risen Christ who seeks out each one of us, wanting to plant the seeds of a new future in the soil of our pain. He comes to replace those thistles and thorns that have torn our lives apart with the buds and blossoms of a new fruitfulness. He wants to help us move from our tears to new beginnings. He wants to make resurrection and healing a reality in our experience.

Answering God's Question

"Why are you crying?" Listen to the question coming to you as you stand with Mary weeping in the garden. Behind the question is the voice of the one who searches for you until he finds you, who calls you by name, and who loves you with a love that will never let you go. As you think about your own tears and the pain that you have been through in your own life, know that you are not alone. Take your time with the question, and as your answer begins to take shape in the depth of your heart, share your response with the risen Christ. You could be crying for any number of reasons.

- I'm crying because I am missing my loved one so much.
- I'm crying because my marriage is in trouble, and I cannot see a way forward.

- I'm crying because divorce has ripped my life apart.
- I'm crying because I am in the dark and don't know what to do.
- I'm crying because my body is in pain, and I cannot find relief.
- I'm crying because of the deep guilt I feel for a past action.
- I'm crying because God seems so far away, and I don't know where to find God.

Maybe your pain is locked away so deeply that you don't even know how to express it. You feel sad but don't know why. This may be the time to speak to a trusted friend or counselor.

As you stand with Mary in the garden, allow her also to represent all those other people who weep today. Think of someone you know who has cried bitterly recently. It could be someone that you know well, someone very close to you; or it could be someone that you have read about in the newspaper or seen on the television screen. In your mind bring the person with you into the presence of Jesus who reaches out to every suffering human being. Hold him or her—their tears, their pain, their sorrow—in your mind and heart as you pray. Let your life become the place where a little of the world's pain can be concentrated and held and shared in the mysterious presence of God who will one day wipe away all tears from all eyes.

As you share the story behind your tears with Christ and hold in your heart the tears of a neighbor, look with Mary into the darkness of the empty tomb. See that the crucified one is no longer there. Let your tears turn into worship as you realize that God has raised Jesus from the dead.

Without resurrection there is no good reason to suppose that you can live beyond your tears. But with the resurrection having taken place, you can weep in the hope that God can lead you beyond your tears toward new beginnings. Without this good news, life makes no sense at all.

Questions for Small Groups

1. Are you comfortable with your own tears?
2. In what ways do you identify with Mary weeping outside the tomb?
3. When have you experienced someone's being a human wailing wall for you? What qualities did this person have?
4. Share one experience when you moved through tears to new beginnings.

Chapter 10

Do You Understand What I Have Done for You?

Some years ago, on Maundy Thursday, I took part in my first-ever foot-washing ceremony. The service was based on the Gospel story where Jesus washed the feet of his disciples. The scene was quite simple. About twenty of us sat in a circle. In the center were basins of water, bars of soap, and some towels. Against a background of gentle music, we listened as someone read John 13. We heard how Jesus took off his outer clothing, wrapped a towel around his waist, poured water into a basin, and began to wash his disciples' feet. Then we knelt at the feet of the person sitting next to us and did the same.

It was a powerful experience. My emotional response took me by surprise. I did not anticipate the feelings of closeness and vulnerability that would accompany this ordinary action. Washing between someone else's toes is a deeply intimate experience. It brought me into a sense of communion with the person whose feet I was washing. I felt that in some profound way, beyond words, I was serving him with God's love. It was quite amazing how such a mundane, down-to-earth action could be so deeply moving. To this day I have not forgotten its effects on my heart and mind.

It was much easier for me to wash another's feet than to let someone wash mine.

What also surprised me was my discomfort at having my feet washed. It was much easier for me to wash another's feet than to let someone wash mine. It took me some time before I could relax, become less tense, and just sit back and enjoy the experience. When I thought about my discomfort afterward, I wondered whether there was a lesson in this for me. Did my reluctance somehow indicate that it was much easier for me to serve than to be served? I think it did and still does. Gradually, however, I was able to overcome my initial unwillingness. In the end I found the experience to be a very tender, healing, and loving one.

Ever since that Maundy Thursday foot-washing experience, this Gospel story has been very special to me. In my office I have a picture that reminds me of it each day. It shows Jesus bent over, kneeling before Peter, and washing his feet. Strikingly, one of Peter's hands rests on Jesus' shoulder, while the other one is raised in protest. This picture confronts me with the same question Jesus asked his disciples after washing their feet. Remember it? "Do you understand what I have done for you?"

This question faces all those who want to walk the Jesus-way. Even though Jesus answered the question to some extent, we do not seem to have grasped its revolutionary significance. Jesus' foot-washing action sharply contradicts the dominant way our society is organized, so we tend to shy away from the question's tough challenge. Foot-washing seems too inconsistent with our culture, too challenging, too radical for ordinary people like you and me. Let us, however, put aside our concerns for the moment and allow Jesus' haunting question to engage us.

The Journey Downward

When Jesus washed the feet of his disciples, he was demonstrating the downward journey, a journey God wants us all to take. To understand what this may mean for our lives, we must step back into Jesus' first-century world. Jesus' society was arranged like a pyramid. At the top were the powerful—the well-off, the well-educated, the well-connected. They were the ones in charge, the ones who ruled, the ones who called the shots. At the bottom were the powerless—the slaves, the uneducated, the alienated. Their job was to serve those at the top. That was the way things worked. It was never the other way around.

One of the ways in which those at the bottom served those above was to wash their feet after a journey or when they came to your home. This menial job was reserved for the lowest servants. Now you can imagine what must have been going through the minds of the disciples when they got together for the Passover supper with Jesus. Who was going to do this job? Certainly none of them was prepared to! When Jesus got up, put the towel around his waist, and began to wash their feet, he was doing the unthinkable. He was identifying with those at the bottom of the pyramid. Quite literally he had gone on a journey downward, acting as a servant.

Not surprisingly, Peter reacted strongly. We can almost hear him saying to himself, *This is not the way things are supposed to work. Our master should not be washing our feet. If we go along with this, what will it mean for us? I will need to readjust all my attitudes, my values, my relationships, the whole way I see the world. I don't want to lower myself like this to anyone. I will not let Jesus wash my feet.* When he said this aloud, Jesus' response to Peter was quite firm: "Unless I wash you, you have no part with me."

When Jesus got up, put the towel around his waist, and began to wash their feet, . . . he was identifying with those at the bottom of the pyramid.

Perhaps like Peter you also resist the idea of a downward journey. In our pyramid society, it is easier and safer to spend time with those nearer the top than to be with those at the bottom. People at the bottom—suffering people, broken people, excluded people—are often quite scary to be with. They remind us of how protected, yet fragile, our lives are. Exposing ourselves to their desperate need can be unsettling. It can also reveal how hard our hearts are, how slow they are to respond to the suffering in our midst.

Yet God continues to call us on this journey downward. Each of us needs to work out what this may mean in our particular situation. At the very least, it implies our involvement with people at the bottom of the pyramid. This involvement could mean forming a relationship with someone who is homeless and destitute or who suffers from a mental illness or who is unemployed or who has Alzheimer's or who is severely handicapped. It may also mean something more. For a doctor friend of mine, it has meant choosing to live among the poorest of the poor and putting his skills at their service. Can you see how Jesus' question, "Do you understand what I have done for you?" challenges us in our pyramid society?

A Pattern to Follow

When Jesus washed the feet of his disciples, he gave us a pattern to follow. Return to the Gospel story. Notice one sentence spoken by Jesus immediately after he had put his teacher's robes back on and sat down. He said to his disciples, "I have given you an example." We would do well to pause and think deeply about these words, and consider their meaning for our lives. They appear nowhere else in any of the four Gospels. There is nothing optional about them. They are clear, direct, and personal. If we want to experience the life God gives, we must follow Jesus' example and wash one another's feet.

Biblical scholars often point out that the word *example* in New Testament Greek means "pattern." I find this insight helpful. Think of a dressmaker who lays out her pattern over fabrics of various colors and designs. She will cut to fit differing body shapes; but each time, the pattern will determine the shape of the dress. Similarly, Jesus has given us the pattern on which to model our lives. Even though we are all different, as dresses are different, this pattern will express itself clearly in each faithful life. It is the pattern of giving ourselves in loving service, just as Jesus did when he washed the disciples' feet.

If we want to experience the life God gives,
we must follow Jesus' example
and wash one another's feet.

Like washing feet, this pattern of loving service usually is expressed in the mundane, the menial, and the messy. I remember once reading a newspaper article about Jonty Rhodes, a world-renowned fielder in cricket, headlined, "No More Jonty to Tidy Up after Nets." The article quoted Eric Simons, the then South African cricket team coach. He was reflecting on what he missed most since Jonty's retirement. It was not his contagious enthusiasm or his lightning-quick running between the wickets or his brilliant catching in the field. Rather it was the way Jonty, at the end of each net practice, would pick up the soft drink bottles and papers lying around and throw them in the trash can.[1]

Jonty's commitment as a Christ-follower is well known. He was one of the senior players on the South African cricket team. Surely, one thinks, this unimportant job would have been done by one of the junior players. Yet Jonty freely chose to do it. I think I know why. His life was in the process of being shaped according to a particular pattern—the pattern of loving service demonstrated for us all when Jesus set aside his robes, poured water into a basin, began to wash the feet of his disciples, and dried them with his towel.

Of course, Jesus' foot-washing example points us toward a greater challenge than merely doing small things for others. It is far more challenging to become a servant in heart and mind, to lay down our lives in the service of the servant-king who gave his life on the cross for every human being. Jesus' action is revolutionary. When he knelt at the feet of his disciples, he was modeling a new way of being; a completely new attitude toward life; a new way of loving and serving our families, our friends, our colleagues, and even our enemies. I have yet to grasp all the implications of his action for my life. Have you?

Upside-Down Authority

When Jesus washed the feet of his disciples, he turned upside down our understanding of the exercise of authority. Consider some of the popular beliefs held by many today about leadership: Leaders must be strong. They must show that they are in charge, in control. They must not reveal weakness or get too close to those "beneath" them, otherwise familiarity could breed contempt; their influence could be compromised. Not surprisingly, when leaders of any kind adopt these beliefs—be they parents, corporate executives, heads of government, teachers, doctors, or even ministers—they often become aloof, distant, and inaccessible.

Jesus invites us to exercise leadership and authority in a radically different way.

However, Jesus invites us to exercise leadership and authority in a radically different way. Look again at the Gospel story. When Jesus washed his disciples' feet, he did not relinquish his authority. He did not deny it or pretend not to have any. He accepted, as applying to himself, the authoritative titles "Lord" and "Master." He often amazed people with the authority with which he spoke and acted. Yet, when we meditate on the picture of him kneeling before Peter, we view a different model of the exercise of authority; this authority finds expression in vulnerability, weakness, and service. We also notice that it can imply closeness, friendship, and intimacy. Upside-down authority is how I describe it—an authority not found in a high position or fancy title but in a towel and a basin.

Several years ago I experienced authority in this upside-down way. The incident stands out in my memory. Our family had just moved into Benoni where I was to take up a new position in the local Methodist congregation. One day, while Debbie and I were loading garden refuse onto a trailer, my new bishop arrived to welcome us. He had just come from an official function and was still dressed for the occasion. Without any fuss, he took off his jacket, rolled up his sleeves, and began to help us in the heat of a hot December sun. To this day, that simple action remains for me a powerful picture of how authority can be expressed in the spirit of Jesus. I will not forget it.

But how do you and I exercise our authority? Do we throw our weight around, or do we lead in a spirit of humility? Do we come across as superior or as persons seeking to serve? These are important concerns, especially if we want to follow Jesus. All of us, to some degree or another, have some form of leadership responsibility: in the home, the workplace, the church, or the wider community. How we lead and serve in these places indicates more than anything else our real answer to Jesus' question, "Do you understand what I have done for you?"

Answering God's Question

Do you understand what I have done for you? How do we begin to answer Jesus' question? We live in a pyramid-shaped society that makes it difficult for us to grasp the full implications of his foot-washing action. It directly opposes the way we are taught the world works. Every day our culture bombards us with messages like: "Work your way to the top." "Look out for yourself." "Show them who's boss." "Be in control." When these ideas and others like them become part and parcel of our thinking, it is very hard to take seriously someone who kneels down and washes feet.

So how can you go about answering the question? Let me offer three simple suggestions:

First of all, if you really do struggle with this Gospel story, it may help to share your feelings with God. Be open and say, "Lord, I do not find it easy to understand what you have done. It seems to go against so much of what I have learned about living in this world. But I do want to try to understand what you meant when you washed your disciples' feet. Will you please shed some light on this moment in your life, so that I may come to see you more clearly, know you more deeply, and follow you more closely." I have found that being honest in this way can often lead us deeper in our relationship with God.

Another way to explore your response to Jesus' question is by trying the following meditation exercise. Take some time to become quiet. Ask God to be near. Read the Gospel story about the foot washing through a few times. When you are familiar with most of its details, put your Bible to one side. Allow the story to come alive in your imagination. Picture yourself sitting with the disciples in the upper room. See Jesus wash their feet. Finally he kneels before you, takes your feet, and places them in his basin. Be aware of your thoughts and feelings as he washes them. When he finishes, he looks up at you and asks, "Do you understand what I have done for you?" Enter into conversation with him from your heart.

My final suggestion involves using the subheadings of this chapter. Take a quick look at each of them again. What do they say to you personally? How do they challenge you personally? What do you understand about the downward journey? about following the pattern of Jesus the servant? about exercising authority in an upside-down way? Share these understandings with God. It may also help to record them in your journal, if you have one. However, remind yourself that understanding alone is not enough. Knowing and doing, theory and action, always go together. Or as Jesus himself put it after he had asked the question, "Now that you know these things, you will be blessed if you do them." What is God challenging you to do? When will you do it?

May you know the blessing that comes from following the foot-washing Christ.

Questions for Small Groups

1. When has someone washed your feet? What was it like?
2. Do you find it easier to serve or to be served? Why?
3. What would a "downward journey" look like for you?
4. What excites or scares you most about following the servant-pattern of Jesus?

NOTES

PREFACE

1. Richard Rohr makes this observation in his foreword to *The Questions of Jesus: Challenging Ourselves to Discover Life's Great Answers,* by John Dear (Colorado Springs, CO: Doubleday Religious Publishing Group, 2004).

CHAPTER 1

1. Frederick Buechner, *The Magnificent Defeat* (New York: HarperCollins Publishers, 1985), 35.
2. William M. Kinnaird, *Joy Comes with the Morning* (Waco, TX: Word Books, 1979), 35.
3. Renée Altson, *Stumbling toward Faith: My Longing to Heal from the Evil That God Allowed* (Grand Rapids, MI: Zondervan, 2004), 171–72.

Chapter 2

1. John R. Claypool, *Opening Blind Eyes* (Nashville, TN: Abingdon Press, 1983), 103.
2. My friend is Alexander Venter. He is also the initiator of Men's Repentance Movement, which led the march. I obtained these details about Lerato from literature that he had put out.

Chapter 3

1. I first came across this legend in the writings of John Powell.
2. Bruce Larson, *What God Wants to Know: Finding Your Answers in God's Vital Questions* (San Francisco: HarperSanFrancisco, 1993), 30.

Chapter 4

1. R. Paul Stevens, *Down-to-Earth Spirituality: Encountering God in the Ordinary, Boring Stuff of Life* (Downers Grove, IL: InterVarsity Press, 2003), 103.

Chapter 5

1. Mike Endicott tells this story in his book *Let Healing Flow, Lord* (Bradford on Avon, UK: Terra Nova Publishers, 2001), 110.

Chapter 6

1. Jean Vanier, *Drawn into the Mystery of Jesus through the Gospel of John* (Mahwah, NJ: Paulist Press: 2004), 40.
2. I first came across this exercise in Gerard W. Hughes' *God in All Things* (London: Hodder & Stoughton, 2004), 86.
3. Ibid., 74.

Chapter 7

1. Eugene H. Peterson, *Subversive Spirituality* (Grand Rapids, MI: Wm. B. Eerdmans Publishing Company, 1997), 8.
2. Personal conversation with Dallas Willard.
3. Joseph F. Girzone, dedication to *Never Alone: A Personal Way to God* (New York: Image Books, 1995), n.p.

Chapter 8

1. Carlos G. Valles, *Let Go of Fear: Tackling Our Worst Emotion* (Liguori, MO: Liguori Publications, 1993).
2. Tom Wright, *John for Everyone: Chapters 1–10*, vol. 1, 2nd ed. (Louisville, KY: Westminster John Knox Press, 2004), 55.

Chapter 9

1. John Goldingay, *Walk On: Life, Loss, Trust, and Other Realities*, rev. ed. (Ada, MI: Baker Academic, 2004), 155.
2. Justice Malala, "Laughter and Forgetting," *Sunday Times* (April 2, 2006).
3. Rob Bell, *Velvet Elvis: Repainting the Christian Faith* (Grand Rapids, MI: Zondervan, 2005), 156–57.

Chapter 10

1. Jermaine Craig, "No More Jonty to Tidy Up after Nets," *Saturday Star* (February 15, 2003).

ABOUT THE AUTHOR

TREVOR HUDSON is married to Debbie, and together they are the parents of Joni and Mark. He has been in the Methodist ministry for over thirty years, spending most of this time in and around Johannesburg. Presently, he is part of the pastoral team at Northfield Methodist Church in Benoni, where he preaches and teaches on a weekly basis. He is deeply committed to the work and ministry of the local congregation and believes strongly that for something to be real it must always be local.

Trevor travels internationally and leads conferences, retreats, and workshops in a number of diverse settings. He has written numerous books, including *A Mile in My Shoes* and *One Day at a Time*. His book *Journey of the Spirit* was awarded Best Christian Book of the Year of 2003 in South Africa.

Trevor's interests include watching sports, walking, discovering new places, reading, and a host of other activities. One of his life's main enjoyments involves hanging out with his family at the local Italian restaurant, enjoying Arrabiata fettuccine followed by ice cream and chocolate sauce.

OTHER UPPER ROOM BOOKS BY TREVOR HUDSON

A Mile in My Shoes: Cultivating Compassion (#9815)

One Day at a Time:
Discovering the Freedom of 12-Step Spirituality (#9913)

Listening to the Groans: A Spirituality for Ministry and Mission (#9933). Written with Stephen D. Bryant.

The Way of Transforming Discipleship
(written with Stephen D. Bryant)
Participant's Book (#9842)
Leader's Guide (#9841)

CPSIA information can be obtained
at www.ICGtesting.com
Printed in the USA
JSHW020937271220
10520JS00005B/10